The Muslim Masquerade

An unveiling of Islam's façade

ISBN: 1-59113-381-5

Published by Jim Croft, 8130 Glades Rd. #327, Boca Raton, Fla. 33434, USA.

Printed in the United States of America.

Booklocker.com, Inc.
2003

The Muslim Masquerade

An unveiling of Islam's façade

Jim Croft

Dedication

This book is dedicated to Abdullah Al Araby, and all like him, who labor to unshackle humanity from the deceptions of Islam.

Acknowledgments

I would like to thank Carolyn Deffenbaugh, Heather Browning, and Bob Rowland for their tireless efforts to help me with the editing of this manuscript. Their command of the English language and proper grammar has proved invaluable.

Explanations

The opinions that are expressed in this book have been garnered through my study of world religions and travels to numerous Islamic nations over the past 45 years. I have spent scores of hours pouring over Muslim literature. I have been investigating reports about international terrorism since 1987.

I owe a special debt of gratitude to Abdullah Al Araby. He is the publisher and primary author of the Islam Review newsletter and its extremely well organized and informative website (www.islamreview.com). Some of the bullet points in this book that feature quotations from the Quran and the Al Bukhari are adaptations from his website and his book *Islam Unveiled.* In such instances wherein the Quran or Hadith are quoted, the punctuations are taken directly from his website. Abdullah Al Araby knows Arabic and has exhaustive knowledge of Muslim literature and clever insights into the facade that veils Islam.

Quotations of the Bible are from the *New Kings James Version.*

Quotations from the Quran are from *The Noble Quran* by Abdullah Yusuf Ali. *

Quotations from the Hadith are from *The Translation of the Meaning of the Sahih Al Bukhari* by Muhammad Muslim Khan, Kazi Publication, Lahore 1979

*Some of the texts from the Quran that are cited may read differently than other updated versions and translations of the Quran. At times, this enigma is spawned by the fact that there has been a great effort among Muslim translators to present Islam as a religion of peace. Therefore, in order to defuse criticisms of

Islam, they often modify the Quranic texts to make the religion appear less primitive and more appealing for Western sensitivities.

Table of Contents

Foreword

Ancient Nineveh was a city full of religion, but God knew what was below the surface and declared:

> "I will lift your skirts over your face,
> I will show the nations your nakedness."
> Nahum 3:5

In this book, Jim Croft has done just that for Islam. He has lifted the religious covering and laid bare the cruelty and the violence, which are the real Islam. Furthermore, in support of his indictment, he has cited the official statements of a whole series of Islamic leaders from Mohammed downwards.

All those who are concerned for the welfare of their nation must come to grips with this rapidly expanding phenomenon of Islam.

Derek Prince
Jerusalem, Israel
December 12, 2001

Introduction

On September the 11th, 2001, Islamic terrorists attacked America and killed thousands of people. Subsequent to this event and numerous other Islamic acts of terrorism, the United States, Great Britain and other democratic nations formed a coalition vowing to end global terrorism. The representatives of this coalition constantly reiterate that the war is not with the Islamic religion. They are careful to state that they believe that Islam is a religion of peace and that the actions of the terrorists are not indicative of all Muslims. This is a politically correct position that is only partially accurate.

Not all Muslims are Arabs

It is accurate to say that not "*all*" Muslims endorse terrorism. This is particularly true of those who appreciate Judeo-Christian values and dwell in genuinely free societies. In this context, being Islamic does not automatically endow a person with inhumane cravings to maim and kill those of other faiths. It is tragically wrong to suspect that everyone with Middle Eastern physical features is a potential terrorist. Not all Arabs are Muslims and not all Muslims are Arabs. Less than 25% of the followers of Islam are of Arabic heritage. In America, 80% of the resident Arabs are actually Christian in their religious affiliation. One of my most treasured friends is a dedicated Evangelical Christian of Palestinian Arab heritage. He has an uncle who is the Christian Orthodox Bishop of Jerusalem. The identification of Muslims should not be reduced to racial features. When it is, a Thai Buddhist can easily be mistaken for an Islamic Indonesian. A group of Nigerian Muslims could easily pass as African Baptists. Armenian Christians may look very similar to Afghani Muslims.

The people who practice the religion of Islam cover the entire spectrum of the nationalities of those who adhere to Christianity. The vast majority of Muslims who live in Christianized nations and a generous portion of those who live in predominantly Islamic states abhor terrorism and simply desire to live their lives in peace. These factors, however, do not vindicate the politically correct assertions that Islam inevitably fosters the qualities of peace. The combination of individual human rights, benevolently effective civil administrations, and tolerant attitudes toward those of other faiths are often rare commodities in Muslim countries.

The purpose of this book is to unveil the façade that the Muslim faith has no culpability in encouraging international terrorism and the misery of masses of people. I will acquaint the reader with insights that are not commonly known about Mohammed and the religion he birthed. It is not my conviction or intention to insinuate that there are not any positive aspects within Islam. There is, however, overwhelming evidence that it has inherent destructive aspects that frequently overshadow the isolated areas wherein it complies with Judeo-Christian values. In this regard it is anything but a religion of peace. The final two chapters deal with two important issues. The first is a call for Muslims to reevaluate Islam as they enter the Twenty-first Century. The second provides an answer for those who assert that the 9/11asault was God's judgment on America.

Chapter 1:
My Observations Of Islam

When I was thirteen-years-old, our family visited the Islamic nation of Libya. I will never forget our guided tour through one of Tripoli's major open markets. Our trek came to an abrupt halt as a man dragged a screaming child, who appeared to be around twelve years of age, across our path. My father asked the Libyan tour guide what was happening. His nonchalant response was that the waif had just been sold into slavery. Thirty-two years later, while en route to Nigeria, I read a *Stars and Stripes* newspaper article. It depicted the plight of thousands of young Muslim girls in Northern Nigeria. It reported that it is a common practice for impoverished families to sell their puberty-aged daughters to become the wives of more affluent men. Many of these children are physically incapable of enduring pregnancy and the birthing process without suffering torn bladders. In Christian societies this condition is routinely corrected by bladder-tack procedures. Not so in Islamic-ruled Northern Nigeria. Its stringent interpretations of Islamic Law dictate that any woman who allows a man, other than her husband, to look upon her nakedness has been defiled and shamed her husband. Therefore, each year hundreds of young girls with leaking bladders are abandoned at clinics to await the remote eventuality of a female physician's attention. The article estimated that at any given time there are hundreds of girls consigned to sit in their own urine awaiting the simple procedure that has the potential to restore them to the husbands who have abandoned them. These experiences led me to suspect that there was something grossly amiss in the religion of Islam. Subsequently, my studies of its holy books and the frequent role of

Muslims in incidences of international terrorism have compelled me to the conviction that it is naïve for anyone to believe the assertion that Islam is a religion of peace.

Fruit determines authenticity

Jesus, when speaking of the false prophets who would appear subsequent to His resurrection, said, *"By their fruits you shall know them"* (Matt. 7:15-20). In this instance the word false is not used to denote the complete absence of truth or genuine sincerity. It pertains to the fruit that is produced in the lives of those who adhere to the teachings of a given spiritual leader. If, as a result of his tutelage, his followers are leading productive harmonious lives, he is a true prophet. If the majority of his followers exemplify oppressive attitudes that enslave them to unproductive lifestyles and incite them to support actions that harm others, he is a false prophet. If this is the criterion for identifying a true from a false prophet, Mohammed and many of Islam's contemporary clerics aptly qualify to be labeled as false prophets. This puts Islam, as a religion, into the dubious position of being labeled as a false religion. There are certainly millions of Muslims who are decent people in spite of the fact that they are involved with a problematic religion. These naïvely offer exemplary devotion toward Allah, fully believing that they are paying homage to a spiritual being that is the same Loving God that Christians and Jews worship.

The word *Islam* means, "*surrender to the will of God*". A Muslim is a person who has surrendered to the will of God by following the religion of Mohammed. Spiritual leaders in the Muslim community are commonly referred to as *Mullahs* and *Imams*. The holy books of Muslims are called the *Quran* and the *Hadith*. The Quran serves as their bible. It is a collection of the revelations that Mohammed alleged were given to him by Allah.

These revelations began in 610AD and ended at Mohammed's death in 632AD. The Hadith is a collection of Mohammed's words and deeds (each called a hadith) according to his wives, relatives, and companions. Next to the Quran, it is the most important part of Islamic law; its teachings are just as binding. Many people have recorded the hadiths of Mohammed in many books. The most popular collection is called the *Sahih Al-Bukhari*, which comes in nine volumes, and contains thousands of hadiths.

Copy cat

Anyone who is familiar with the Bible and reads either the Quran or the Hadith can discern that Mohammed was familiar with Judaism and Christianity and that he borrowed generously from their writings. Mohammed made the self-aggrandizing claim that he was God's (Allah's) final messenger with divine insights and an anointing that eclipsed those of his predecessors, Abraham, Moses, the New Testament's Apostles, and Jesus. According to the Christian Bible, Mohammed can be identified as a deceived deceiver who was operating under the influence of a spirit of antichrist. The prefix *anti* of the word *antichrist* can mean *in place of as well* as *against*. The word *Christ* is defined as *the anointed one of God*. Therefore, a reasonable expanded definition of the word *antichrist* might read, *one who is operating in an anointing that is a substitute for the true anointing* (Heb. 1:1-3 & 1 John 4:1-3). Mohammed espoused teachings that denied the divine Sonship of Jesus. In 1 John 2:22, it says that anyone who denies the Father and the Son is a liar of the antichrist. The Muslim mosque in Jerusalem is called the *Mosque of Omar*. It bears an Arabic inscription that defies the Father and Son relationship between God and Jesus. It says, *"Allah has no son"*. Mohammed also denied Jesus' death by crucifixion. He claimed that Allah told him that Jesus was elevated to heaven before His physical death. Muslims promote their Prophet's postdated revelations as superior to those of Jesus and His Apostles.

In recent years Islam has launched a global campaign to lure people of other faiths into its ranks. Its strategy is cunningly deceptive. In Christian nations Muslims subtly cloak Islam in the guise of being closely akin to Christianity. They boast Quranic verses that mention Jesus and His miracles while they hide the fact that they deny His divinity and His atoning crucifixion, death, and physical resurrection. Their rhetoric often employs Christian terms such as salvation, justification, and sanctification. The truth is these terms do not have any historical precedent in Muslim teachings. In many instances, they have adopted a slanted freestyle method of translating certain sections of the Quran in order to defuse the appearance of contempt for Christians and Jews. Here is an example from the new French translation of the Quran in regard to the Jews. It reads, "*The people of Israel will be twice destroyed as an innocent victim, and God will reward them by elevating them to great heights*". The old translation reads just the opposite. "*The people of Israel, after sowing corruption twice on earth for the purpose of dominating other people, will push themselves up into a position of extreme power before being punished by God*".

Pillars of Islam

There are five pillars to the Islamic faith among moderate Muslims and six among the radicals. I will list all six and add the ways in which each differs from Christianity in parentheses.

- *Shahada* is their profession of faith that states, "*There is no other God but Allah, and Mohammed is the messenger of*

Allah." – (Christian conversion rests solely on repentance from one's sins and the revelation and confession that Jesus is the Son of God who was raised from the dead.)

- *Salat* is praying five times daily while kneeling toward Mecca, Saudi Arabia. – (Christians are encouraged to simply worship in spirit and in truth from any position at anytime and anywhere.)
- *Sawm* is fasting during the daylight hours of the month of Ramadan. – (For Christians fasting is an optional discipline.)
- *Zakat* is almsgiving. – (Christians are encouraged to tithe and give freewill offerings. Neither of these is mandatory for salvation.)
- *Hajj* is a pilgrimage to Mecca at least once in one's lifetime. – (Christianity has no official holy city that one is obligated to visit. Trips to historical sites in Israel are an optional privilege.)
- *Jihad* is the Quranic sanction of holy war as a religious duty to spread Islam. – (Coercion is unacceptable to Christians and the Lord they serve. They propagate the Gospel by preaching Christ to those who have an interest in Christianity.)

Two Arabic words

The word *Islam* has connections with two Arabic words. One is *tasleem*, which means, *"surrender"* or *"submission"*. The other is *salaam*, which by definition is closely related to the Hebrew word *shalom*. It conveys peace with God and one's self, harmonious interpersonal relationships, and the blessings of God. These graces are, more often than not, infrequent experiences for those living in Muslim-controlled nations. When compared to countries that are under predominant Christian influence, there are significant indications that wherever the Islamic faith is the predominant spiritual influence within a nation, that nation is rendered incapable of producing anything akin to the peaceful harmony of *salaam*. Islamic nations have disproportionate numbers of reports of human rights violations against women, children and those of other religions. These countries have high illiteracy rates, excessive infant mortality statistics, and low productivity in the fields of science and technology in comparison with nations that are under predominant Christian influence. When the threat of global Islamic terrorism is thrown into the equation, it denotes that Islam is most definitely not a religion that inspires innovative creativity in science and technology, harmonious interfaith relationships, and world peace.

Egotistical claims

The source of these problems that reside within most Muslim-governed countries is found in several interrelated aspects of the nature of the Islamic religion. First, the Islamic holy books present the egotistical claims of Mohammed concerning his superiority to preceding spiritual leaders and the superiority of Muslims to non-Muslims. Some entity, professing to be Allah, the God of all creation, often gave Mohammed contradictory revelations about issues such as war, human rights, and the treatment of non-Muslims. These revelations were recorded in Islam's holy books and became Muslim Law. The Quran and the Hadith insist that absolute obedience to these Laws will lead true believers into lifestyles that will please Allah. Secondly, Islam, like all religions, has a portion of adherents that are hard-core extremists. In Islamic nations, even when the moderates are in the majority, the extremists are far more proactive and politically powerful. Their radical clergymen emphasize the intolerant laws as much as they do the more rational ones. This incites their followers to organize public demonstrations that demand that the whole society legalistically adhere to all of the laws as a means of invoking the blessings of Allah on the nation. They authoritatively proclaim that they know all there is to know about what Mohammed said and what the will of Allah is for everyone else. All of this intimidates the moderates that just want to live and let live. They melt under the intensity and give lip service to whatever the extremists are prescribing. This leads the non-Muslim world to perceive the Muslim world as inhabited primarily by dangerous, unreasonable, fanatical radicals. Simply stated, if the teachings of Mohammed and the inflammatory rhetoric of fundamentalist clerics were extracted from the hearts and minds of people in Muslim-controlled nations, the negative generalizations of non-Muslims would be defused and Muslims would be liberated to rise to their full potential as human beings. The same mental and spiritual surgery would cause Islamic terrorists to lose the primary motivation for their actions.

The ex-Muslim, Muhammad bin Abdullah, voiced a similar opinion in Ibn Warraq's book, *Leaving Islam.* *"It is indeed dangerous to humankind that nothing can stop Islam from breeding cruel killers time and time again. That is because many of the Prophet's deeds and Koranic instruction are always alive there to act as fertile ground for breeding killers".*

Chapter 2:
Muslims Flourish In Christian Nations

Westernized nations are inhabited by millions of Islamic citizens representing most every racial group. Many of them are friendly, peace-loving people that quietly live their lives as they follow their faith. When they are privileged to live in societies that have infrastructures that are built upon Judeo-Christian values and political climates that are unencumbered by religious fanaticism, they flourish. Significant numbers of their men and women, when given equal educational and vocational opportunities, make valuable contributions to the business communities and the fields of medicine and technology within the respective Western democracies in which they reside.

Unfortunately, this is not the case within the Islamic-governed nations. These countries do not enjoy a separation of religion and state. The clergy rules and the civil authorities enforce their policies. Education is often restricted to males, and the scholastic institutions are commonly antiquated and ill equipped. Those that promote Islam often boast of its "*Golden age*". During this period, from 700 through 1200AD, Europe was in the Dark Ages. The Middle East and Asian nations that had been conquered by Islamic Jihad (holy war or struggle) led the world as they continued to make advances in the disciplines of literature, science and math. There are, however, many scholars that contend that these advances were a continuation of the groundwork that had been laid by Jews, Persians and Christians prior to the arrival of the Muslims. This is supported by the reality that by the end of the Twelfth Century, the advances ceased in the Muslim world. In contrast, progress was restored in Christianized nations during the

Renaissance and continued through the Industrial Revolution into the high-tech achievements of the current era. Islamic countries were left sitting in the sand. One would be hard pressed to cite a single original medical, industrial, or technological innovation that has come forth from an Islamic-governed nation without the under girding of Western influence and education. During the past five hundred years Islamic nations have not produced one contribution to science, technology or industry in a stand-alone manner. They have no Wright Brothers, Henry Fords or Dr. Jonas Salks. Students from the global community are not lined up to apprehend visas to study at the universities of Saudi Arabia and Afghanistan. The foreign embassies of Christian countries are flooded with visa applications from Muslims that are seeking opportunities to live in the fertile environments that are built on Judeo-Christian values. It would seem that if Islam really had so much to offer, we would see people from Christian nations flocking to get work and educational visas in Islamic states.

DNA is not the problem

What caused the cessation of academic progress in the nations that were conquered by Islam? Did some DNA mutation kick in that caused people's intelligence to be altered? This could not be the case because many of the same nationalities prove to be brilliant in settings that are founded on principles other than interpretations of Mohammed's teachings. The finger of guilt points toward the Muslim religion and the teachings of its clerics. The cessation of innovation was caused by the rule of Islam from 700 through 1200AD. It took five hundred years for it to finally take hold and totally stifle the progress of the nations that were under its influence.

In short, you can tell the value of a religion by observing the plight of nations that have lived under its influence for an extended period. If a religion has merit, it will inspire creativity from those that adhere to it. South Korea was predominantly Buddhist prior to its war with Communist North Korea in 1950. Christian nations defended South Korea, and subsequently the influence of Christianity has steadily increased. Even though its economy was devastated by the war, it has risen from the ash heaps and now has a gross national product (GNP) that dwarfs those of the oil rich Islamic-controlled nations. Christianized South Korea's GNP for 2001 was $764.8 billion, while Islamic Saudi Arabia's GNP for 2000 was $232 billion and Communist North Korea's GNP was $21.8 billion. In contrast Haiti, before its independence from France in the Eighteenth Century, had a greater gross national product than the thirteen original American colonies combined. Voodoo mixed with Catholicism set in, and it is now the most impoverished nation in the Western Hemisphere. Many people of East Indian heritage have engineered some of the most advanced technologies in the computer sciences. Yet, Hinduism has reduced their homeland to a nation where scores of thousands starve daily as eatable cows roam the streets. In the same manner, the Muslim sheiks of the Middle East would be riding on camels, rather than in air-conditioned Mercedes, if it were not for the oil drilling technology of Christian nations. Whenever Islam is the primary focus of a government, the majority of its citizens languish in an abased existence. If those same people immigrate to a democratic society, where the pursuit of happiness is primary and their degree of religious expression is optional, they are apt to flourish.

There are sources that can validate much of what has been stated in this book's introduction and this chapter. Anyone that searches the Internet for websites dealing with the issues of terrorism, human rights violations, slavery, child-labor law infractions, and crimes against women will discover that Islamic nations are cited with a disproportionate number of abuses. The 2003 edition of the World Almanac reveals some alarming statistics in relation to infant mortality and illiteracy rates. The following is an accumulative comparison of the rates of Muslim nations and Christian democracies.

- The average infant mortality rates in Islamic states run from a low of 30 in 1,000 births to a staggering 160 out of 1,000. Predominately Christian democracies have statistics that average around 5 out of 1,000 births.
- The reported illiteracy rates under the rule of Muslims run from a low of 20% to a high of 74%. These figures may not be accurate, as women are not always included in the reports. The illiteracy rates in Europe, the United Kingdom, and on the North American continent run under 3%.

Chapter 3:
Jihad

The Islamic terrorist attacks of September the 11th, 2001 and their subsequent acts of terrorism spurred the major television networks to air documentaries on the religion of Islam and interviews with intellectuals that were alleged to be authorities on the subject. The documentaries that were filmed and narrated by journalists were candid, and they posed pungent questions in relation to the nature of the Muslim faith. The intellectuals were not given to the same degree of objectivity. More often than not, they presented the religion within the context of how it can be experienced in the ideal environment of a free democratic society. They led the viewers to believe that there are no differences between Muslims living in Christianized nations that can choose the degree of their adherence to Islamic Law and those living in Islamic states that do not have the same options. They failed to inform the viewers about the Muslim worldview that divides humanity into two opposing halves. One side *Dar es Salaam*, which means *The House of Peace*, is the zone where Islam rules. The other side *Dar el Harb*, which means *The House of War*, is the war zone that is occupied by non-Muslims. The Muslim worldview dictates that war will continue between these two sections of humanity until the supremacy of Islam is fully established throughout the world. The armchair theologians unequivocally asserted that Islam was a religion of peace and that the terrorists' attacks were a shocking anomaly. They cunningly attempted to defuse any notion that the behavior of the terrorists was a legitimate expression of Jihad or Islamic holy war. Jihad, it was explained, primarily means to struggle with one's sinful inclinations to rebel against the will of Allah. It was insisted that Jihad is only used as a synonym for holy war in the context of defense and never as a term for hostile actions as a means of offense. The words of Mohammed, the facts of history and the protests of Muslims in non-Western nations belie their heady assertions that Jihad is simply a benign spiritual term. The rioting crowds of Muslims that chant "*Jihad*" over and over indicate that the word has undergone an idiomatic transformation in their understanding. Even if its original, antiquated meaning was "*struggle*", it is an idiom today that primarily means "*holy war that endorses terrorism*".

The Real Islam

In the book *Leaving Islam*, Muhammed bin Abdullah offered his insights, as an ex-Muslim, about the true nature of Islam. *"I faced the truth of the mess of the Koran and hadith. The Koran does not contain a single humane teaching that was not here before Islam. Mankind will not lose a single moral precept if Islam is not there tomorrow. After consulting the Koran, the hadith, the Prophet's biography, and Islamic history for years, with a guarded, open mind, I related the past to the present. People tried reforming Islam; it never worked. Again and again, Islam was mortgaged in the hands of killer leadership, while the rest of the Muslim world only said, "this is not real Islam".*

"Once again, the dual character of Islam became clear. Islam has two sets of teeth, like elephants. One is ivory, which makes it elegant and majestic; the other set of teeth is hidden inside its jaws, and is used to chew and crush. All those sweet peace talks of Islam relate to the time and place of weak Islam in early years. But whenever and wherever Muslims were and are strong, they have another set of cruel laws and conduct. Tell me why the

national flags of many Muslim countries have swords on them – a sword is not for shaving beards, it's only for killing".

Rejoicing over tragedy

When the news that thousands of American civilians, and those of 86 other nations, had been killed in the terrorist attacks on the World Trade Center in Manhattan and Washington's Pentagon reached Israel, Palestinian Muslims rejoiced in the streets. Egyptians in the cafés of Cairo were filmed congratulating one another over the triumph of their fellow believers. Thousands of Muslims in numerous countries vowed to support the Taliban of Afghanistan and Iraq's Hussein regime in Jihad against the evil Satan, America. A poll of Pakistan's Muslim population revealed that 83% supported the terrorist Osama Bin Laden. None of these actions denote the attitudes of people that embrace a religion that values peace. It is atypical behavior for people that have spiritual leaders that have taught them tolerance. Boisterous public protest is the primary vehicle for citizens in Muslim lands to voice their approval or disapproval of world events. If the majority of Muslims really abhor terrorism, why are there not massive protests to counteract the riotous demonstrations of those that applaud the exploits if Islam's international terrorists?

It is naïve to claim that only extremists are involved. Every religion, including Christianity, has its share of extremists. However, you don't see thousands of Protestants rejoicing in the streets of Germany when members of the IRA bomb a British military installation in Belfast, Ireland. When the British retaliate, there are never any reports of massive numbers of Christians in scores of nations vowing to join their Irish brothers in a holy crusade against British citizens living wherever they might be found. Several years ago, after a demonized anti-abortion advocate assassinated an abortionist doctor in Pensacola, Florida, the Christian community did not applaud him. Fundamentalist pastors across America did not lead their congregations in protests when he was indicted for murder. No one could routinely find instances where conservative disciples of Jesus Christ in multiple countries would promote such a person as a role model for the youths of their churches. Not so in Islam. Hundreds of mosques and educational facilities display posters of Bin Laden like Christians display pictures of Jesus' Last Supper. There are continuous reports of thousands of Muslims from every sector of the world voicing their willingness to join the terrorist Bin Laden in his Jihad against America.

The Moderate Muslim Myth

Inevitably, whenever Islam is mentioned in a negative context, many quickly challenge that only a small minority are dangerous radicals and that the majority are harmless moderates. I believe that the facts disprove this oversimplified distinction. There is a two edged-sword of Islam. One edge is terrorism and the other is the subtle process that leads to Islamization. The latter edge is comprised of moderates that, wittingly and unwittingly, work hand-in-hand with the terrorists in America. The truth of this is hidden in a chilling statement that a leading Islamic spokesman made to the Archbishop of Izmir, Turkey during an Islam - Christian dialogue meeting. *"Thanks to your democratic laws we will invade you; thanks to our religious laws we will dominate you."*

Unfair Tactics

Here is how it works. The extremists commit acts of terrorism against us. The moment that our authorities begin to investigate

Islamic communities for hidden terror cells and supporters, the moderates cry "*constitutional foul*". They charge us with religious and race discrimination. Thus they use our democratic laws against us. This thwarts our investigative efforts to defend ourselves and opens the door for more terrorists to invade our shores. The success of moderates in manipulating our system enables them to be perceived as a valuable voting block by prospective candidates for public office. This multiplies their potential to have ever-increasing influence over our government. Few Americans understand that Islam inherently demands what is called a "*sacral government*". The vernacular for this is a "*Church-State*" form of rule. Islam is a religion that insists that its laws have dominant influence in the affairs of a nation's government (See Quran 3:85, 12:40). In reality, a moderate Muslim doesn't qualify as a devoted Muslim unless he concurs with the Quran and every Islamic law. Fundamentalist Muslims don't consider a Muslim who voices complaints against other Muslims as a true believer. This is why there has been an absence of public Muslim protests about the Islamic terrorist crimes that have been perpetrated within our nation.

Our politically correct news media and Muslim activist spokesmen have conditioned us with perceptions that may contain significant elements of inaccuracy. They assert that the majority of the citizens living in Islamic states are harmless moderates that have no sympathy for the terrorists.

Osama's secret admirers

This is belied by reports that post 9/11 the first name of Bin Laden, "*Osama*", has attained a favored name status for newborn male infants in a dozen or more Muslim countries. In some nations seven out of ten baby boys are the namesakes of the terrorist. Unless only radicals are bearing children, there are two other possibilities. Many moderates are curiously enamored with and supportive of Bin Laden's exploits. Or, the moderation of moderates has been exaggerated.

It is my conviction that in reality there are three types of Muslims. They are the radicals, the moderates, and the westernized. The majority of those inhabiting America are likely the westernized variety. These love our nation and have wholeheartedly embraced our Judeo-Christian values.

Westernized Muslims embrace Judaic-Christian values

They understand that the opportunities that are afforded them here could never be realized in a Muslim-ruled country. For these, the pursuit of happiness is primary, their religion a meaningless coincidence of birth. In my estimation there is only one variety of Muslims who we are guaranteed would never wittingly aid and abet terrorists or cooperate with schemes to Islamize us. It is the westernized. Rarely could any member of this group be unwittingly lured into schemes of duplicity, as they have learned to regard fellow Muslims with suspicion.

Jihad, holy war, was the primary vehicle that was used to spread the Muslim faith through the ancient world. From 632 through 1514AD Islamic armies raped and pillaged their way from Medina, Saudi Arabia to Iran and then onto the borders of German and French-speaking Europe. The nations pictured in our Bible maps, that were the cradle of the Christian faith, have few Gospel-proclaiming churches left. Mosques have replaced the churches. These countries include Israel, Jordan, Syria and Turkey. The nations of North Africa, stretching from Egypt westward through Libya and Algeria and on to Morocco, were once bastions of Christianity. They all fell under the crescent moon of Islam by the

Tenth Century. The present-day descendants of the early Christians, unlike their forefathers, are not filled with the Holy Spirit. They are languishing as Muslims in the grip of the anti-Christ spirit of Islam. The seven cities addressed by the Spirit of Christ in the book of Revelation that were once flourishing with saved, baptized Christians, have been Islamized. Most of the conquered were given the choice of conversion or the sword. Conversion then and now is accomplished by repeating the Shahada three times, "*There is no God but Allah, and Mohammed is the prophet of Allah*". During this period Christians, Jews, and other minorities that did not convert and managed to escape the sword became second-class citizens. Muslims called them *Ahl-al-Dhimma* or *Dhimmis*. This *Dhimmitude* status was, and remains to this day, synonymous with discrimination. They had to pay a special tax, wear distinct clothing, and were denied the right to have a voice in politics.

Shameful crusades

When the subject of Jihad is mentioned, well-read Muslims often bring up one of the saddest periods in Christian history. It is the era in which Christendom, like much of the Muslim world of today, primarily consisted of nations that were religious states. During this era, Christianity had its own form of Jihad. The Church-State armies of Europe attempted to advance the influence of the Cross of Christ through holy wars. From 1095 through 1464 AD, the Church-State governments of Europe initiated barbarous campaigns, called Crusades, to free the Middle East from the grip of Islamic infidels. The Crusaders were no less cruel than the Muslim Jihad warriors had been when they conquered the same geography. The Crusades, however, lasted less than four hundred years. On the other hand, Jihad has never ceased to be an

Islamic tool to increase its influence. A brief glimpse into the era that spawned the Crusades will demonstrate that Christianity has more dissimilarities than similarities with Islam.

The administration of the Roman emperor Constantine, around 300AD, marked a strategic departure from the Church's traditional method of evangelization. Up until that juncture, the Church had been faithful to Jesus' words that His disciples would not fight because His kingdom was not of this world (Jn. 18:35-37). Christians brought sinners to the cross through their preaching and their exemplary corporate witness of the imitation of the love and meekness of Christ amidst a hostile environment. Constantine, being an ambitious opportunist, perceived Christianity as a vehicle to strengthen Rome's might by uniting the empire under a single monotheistic religion. He accurately assessed that this move would serve a dual role. It would defuse the competition for prominence that existed amongst the numerous polytheistic factions within the empire. More importantly, it would arm his troops with the fervor of religious purpose as they went forth to conquer the world. Sadly, the Church welcomed this as a means of relief from generations of rigorous persecution. The Church joined hands with the secular state, and its mode of evangelization became tainted. Subsequent to Constantine's reign, the Roman Empire collapsed. Nonetheless, the partnership of the State and Church in Christendom thrived. It marched through Western Europe century after century, subduing aboriginal tribes and kingdoms from province to province. The aboriginal groups within the Latin, Germanic, Scandinavian, Gaul, and Anglo-Saxon territories were given the option of conversion or persecution. These respective groups evolved into nations that had governments that predominately complied with and enforced the directives of the Church. For the next twelve hundred years only isolated groups of Christians and clergymen demonstrated any evidence that they understood that authentic conversion is effected only when it is a choice of conscience rather than coercion. Most Christian clerics and civil rulers were austere figures that had no qualms about assisting the process of spiritual regeneration with the sword of force. There were times when the Lord intervened and brought revivals that helped spread the authentic Gospel of Christ. These, however, seldom continued to bear fruit into successive generations, as the churches that took in the newly converted were simply not places where spiritual growth could flourish.

Needful reformation

The winds of change did not begin to blow in Christendom until around 1526AD as Martin Luther began declaring, "*the just shall live by faith*", and the Protestant Reformation was launched. Subsequently, over the next several centuries increasing numbers of Churchmen gradually put aside heavy emphasis on Old Testament Laws as a means of righteousness and began to preach New Testament conversion through faith. The influence of the Church over states waned, and calls for Christian armies to conquer infidels ceased.

It is at this juncture that Christianity has two strategic dissimilarities with Islam. First, Islam has never had a monumental reformation that significantly altered its mode of operation. Secondly, the Islamic Quran and the Old Testament of the Christian Bible depict an all-powerful God that demands that the entire earth obey His laws and His prophets. Both of these books contain references to spiritual leaders calling their constituents to holy wars in which the genocide of the enemies of

God was encouraged. The dissimilarity is that the Christian Bible has a New Testament and the Quran does not.

The New Testament represents a shift in focus within God's dealings with the human race. It is called the *Dispensation of Grace*, and it is a radical change from the Old Testament's *Dispensation of the Law*. Under the Dispensation of Grace complete obedience to a set of religious laws and regulations is not required as a means of securing a degree of righteousness that will please God. Having the faith to believe that Jesus completely fulfilled all of the laws of God on behalf of all who would put their trust in Him bestows the gift of righteousness to Christians. The New Testament does not infer that earthly nations can become holy by demanding that all citizens obey religious and civil laws as dictated by political clergymen. God now has only one holy nation, and it is the universal Church. Its citizens are scattered among every nation, tribe, and tongue. The New Testament encourages them to view the secular governments of the nations in which they reside as ordained by God, regardless of the presence or absence of spiritual devotion within the civil administrations of their respective nations.

Graceless Islam

Islam has no Dispensation of Grace. Muslims are still under the laws of Allah as perceived by Mohammed up until his death in 632AD. Holy war to convert infidels by the sword of coercion is still in effect. Jihad that includes genocide and terrorism is routinely encouraged by many of Islam's clerics. Millions of Muslims will be discontent until the nations of their residence surrender to the will of Allah and the crescent moon of Islam is flown over every country on the planet. These preceding statements will now be validated by quotations from the Quran, the hadiths found in the Sahih Al-Bukhari and the words of contemporary Muslim spiritual and political leaders.

The following is an excerpt taken from a statement issued by Osama Bin Laden's spokesman, Abu Ghaith. He opened with a line from the Quran instructing Muslims not to take Jews and Christians as their leaders, saying that would make them part of them. *"O ye who believe! Take not the Jews and the Christians for your friends and protectors. They are but friends and protectors to each other. And he amongst you that turns to them (for friendship) is one of them. Allah guideth not a people unjust."* - Quran Surah 5:51

Bin Laden's spokesman: *"Allah says fight, for the sake of Allah and to uphold the name of Allah. The American interests are everywhere all over the world. Every Muslim has to play his real and true role to uphold his religion and his nation in fighting, and Jihad is a duty."*

These are sayings of Mohammed as recorded in the Islamic holy books. It is undeniable that these passages support terrorism and Jihad.

- *"Strike terror (into the hearts of) the enemies of Allah and your enemies."* - Quran Surah 8:60
- *"Fight (kill) them (non-Muslims), and Allah will punish (torment) them by your hands, cover them with shame."* - Quran Surah 9:14
- *"I will instill terror into the hearts of the unbelievers, smite ye above their necks and smite all their finger-tips off them. It is not ye who slew them; it was Allah."* - Quran Surah 8:12
- Mohammed once was asked: *"What is the best deed for the Muslim next to believing in Allah and His Apostle?"* His

answer was: *"To participate in Jihad in Allah's cause."* - Al Bukhari, Vol. 1:25

• Mohammed was quoted as saying: *"I have been ordered to fight with the people till they say, none has the right to be worshipped but Allah".* - Al Bukhari, Vol. 4:196

• Mohammed also said, *"The person who participates in (Holy Battles) in Allah's cause and nothing compels him to do so except belief in Allah and His Apostle, will be recompensed by Allah either with a reward or booty (if he survives), or will be admitted to paradise (if he is killed)."* - Al Bukhari, Vol. 1:35.

• When the prophet of Islam started preaching his new religion in Mecca, he was conciliatory to Christians and Jews. He told them: *"We believe in what has been sent down to us and sent down to you, our God is the same as your God."* - Quran Surah 29:45

• This attitude changed completely after he gained strength. Supposedly, Allah changed his mind and told Mohammed to *"Fight those who believe not in Allah nor the last day... Nor acknowledge the religion of truth (Islam), (even if they are) of the people of the Book (Christians and Jews), until they pay the Jizya (taxes) with willing submission, and feel themselves subdued."* (Quran Surah 9:29) Muslim activists do not tell prospective converts and the press that the conciliatory verses that Mohammed wrote while in Mecca were later nullified by the hostile ones written in Medina.

• Islamic extremists use Mohammed's phrase, *lie in wait for them with every stratagem*, to justify terrorism as an orthodox tactic of Jihad. *"Fight and slay the Pagans wherever ye find them, and seize them, beleaguer them, and lie in wait for them in every stratagem (of war)."* - Quran Surah 9:5

The PLO

Most of the citizens of non-Muslim countries are unaware of a number of factors about the Palestine Liberation Organization's Jihad to drive the Jews from Israel. The youngsters that are portrayed as brave freedom fighters as they throw rocks at Israeli soldiers armed with guns are not without vested interests. Through subsidies from Saudi Arabia, Iran, and Iraq, the PLO guarantees them scholarships if they desire education beyond secondary school. If one of them happens to be killed, his family, like those of suicide bombers, will receive generous financial remuneration.

The Jews did not invade Palestine, before it became the state of Israel, and wrest it from the control of the Palestinian Muslims. There had been a continuing Jewish presence there since the time that God gave them the land thirty-five hundred years ago. Up until the Second Century it had always been known as Israel or Judea, the home of the Jews. In 135AD a Jewish leader named Bar Kokohba led a revolt against Rome. This enraged the Emperor Hadrian, and he vindictively decided to wipe out the name and memory of Israel. Therefore he renamed Israel after their age-old enemies, the Philistines and called it *Syria et Philistia.* The area became known as Palestine due to the fact that the word *Palestine* is a corruption of the familiar biblical term *Philistine.* Over the centuries Muslim and Christian Arabs filtered into the area and lived alongside of the Jews. These referred to themselves as Palestinians because they lived in the area that had been labeled Palestine. In the Twentieth Century, the persecuted Jews of Europe began to return to their homeland in greater numbers. This increased the tensions between the Palestinians and the Jews that occupied the region. The area was under the control of the Syrians. Then on January 3, 1919, Emir Feisal of Syria signed an agreement with the Jews wherein he renounced all claims to the area known as Palestine. He said that it should be the territory of the Jews.

Jews purchased the land

After this period there were Arabs that claimed title to large portions of the land. The Zionist Jews saw a need to secure the fact of their rights to settle in the area, so they purchased a substantial portion of it. Between 1933 and 1935, one hundred sixty-four thousand Jewish immigrants from Europe paid absentee Arab landowners $20,000,000 for a rocky, sandy and swampy area within the borders of present-day Israel. With God-inspired skill they transformed their acreages into a green, productive land for the first time in hundreds of years. In 1937, it was the intent of the Arabs to secure a big Arab state outside of the area of ancient Judea, leaving little Israel (Judea) for the Jews. Their slogan then was "*Arabia for the Arabs and Judea for the Jews*". The creation of a separate Arab state never materialized, and the Jews and Palestinians have been in varying intensities of conflict ever since.

It is interesting to note that even though there has been a continuing presence of Palestinian Arabs living in Israel for hundreds of years that Arab academics disclaim the existence of Palestine as a part of Arab history. In 1946 the Arab historian Professor Hitti testified that there is absolutely no mention of a Palestine anywhere in Arab history. Jerusalem is not mentioned once in the Quran, but it is mentioned over seven hundred times in the Bible. In 1977 the PLO leader Zuhair Mohsen stated that the Palestinian people did not exist as a separate entity and that they all belonged to the Arab people. He further stated that the establishment of a Palestinian state was just a ploy to continue their struggle against Israel in the cause of Arab unity.

Chapter 4:
Mohammed's Views On Human Rights Issues

Slavery is an ancient practice that still exists today. It is outlawed in most Muslim countries, but there are all too many instances where authorities turn a blind eye to the slave trade in their respective jurisdictions. According to United Nations reports and numerous Internet slavery websites, the Islamic nations of Mauritania, Pakistan and the Sudan actively engage in slave trade and ownership. Any Muslim that desires justification for slavery will find encouragement in the sayings and actions of Mohammed. The writer Ibn Qayyim al-Jawziyya is regarded as a primary authority and reliable source among the students of Islamic religion. In his book *Zad al-Ma'ad*, he lists the names of twenty-six male slaves that were owned by Mohammed. *"These are the names of Muhammad's male slaves: Yakan Abu Sharh, Aflah, 'Ubayd, Dhakwan, Tahman, Mirwan, Hunayn, Sanad, Fadala Yamamin, Anjasha al-Hadi, Mad'am, Karkara, Abu Rafi', Thawban, Ab Kabsha, Salih, Rabah, Yara Nubyan, Fadila, Waqid, Mabur, Abu Waqid, Kasam, Abu' Ayb, Abu Muwayhiba, Zayd Ibn Haritha, and also a black slave called Mahran."* - (Part 1, pp. 114-116)

When Mohammed was alive, he encountered a fellow Muslim that was a pedophile. The man had freed a young boy that he had kept as a sexual partner. When Mohammed heard what happened, he auctioned the boy and sold him for 800 derhams to another Muslim (Sahih Moslem. Vol. 7, page 83).

Blacks of Christian heritage often convert to Islam due to their disappointment over the fact that many of the colonial slave owners professed to be Christians and there are still elements of racial prejudice within the Church. Some of these new converts are intrigued with the deceptive claims of Muslims. They are often led to believe that Mohammed was a black man and that Islam originated in Africa. These assertions are false and are part and parcel with the duplicity that is characteristic of many that follow Islam.

The majority of the slaves that were imported to America came from West Africa, as opposed to East Africa. It was an absolute rarity for white Europeans or Americans to attempt to raid African villages to kidnap individuals for the slave trade. They did not need to because Africans of different tribes had been enslaving one another for centuries. The chiefs of these tribes would often sell their captives to Muslim slave traders that would transport them to the various West African seaports. This made them more accessible to the white slave ships that would make a quick turn around to transport the slaves to the Caribbean Islands and the Americas. Saudi Arabia, where Islam was founded, is on the Asian continent. Black Africa and Yellow Asia are two different continents that are separated by the Red Sea. The Muslim faith did not spread into Africa until many years after the death of its founder. He was an Arab-Asian, as was the first generation of his disciples. The Holy books of Islam describe Mohammed as a white man.

Mohammed was not black

"While we were sitting with the Prophet, a man came and said, 'who amongst you is Mohammed?' We replied, 'this white man reclining on his arm.'" (Al Bukhari, Vol. 1:63) In Volume 2:122 it refers to Mohammed as a "*white person*", and in Vol. 2:141 we are told that when Mohammed raised his arms, *"the whiteness of his armpits became visible"*.

Anyone of Black-African heritage that embraces Islam in hope of escaping from race prejudice and attaining greater opportunities for freedom is choosing an inept haven. If he visited Mauritania, Pakistan or the Sudan, he would likely see contemporary slavery. According to an American State Department news release dated May 26th, 1993, African Muslims are kidnapping their African Christian brothers in Sudan, butchering the weak and selling the healthy as slaves. Mohammed not only owned black slaves, but he also spoke of blacks in a denigrating, prejudicial manner. He called them "raisin heads." - Al Bukhari, Vol. 1:662 & Vol. 9:256. Even in modern times, in Saudi Arabia, the homeland of Islam, the common word for the color black is *Abd*. It also means, "*slave*". America can be faulted for endorsing slavery over one hundred years ago. But, well over two hundred thousand Union American soldiers gave their lives to free the blacks. No Muslim nation has ever initiated a civil war specifically to free black slaves. There are still pockets of oppressive discrimination in the United States and other Western democracies, but it is illegal and waning. Under Islam a number of national governmental authorities turn a deaf ear to the cries of enslaved people of various races, including thousands that are black.

Barbarism

According to the Cable News Network there are some Islamic fundamentalist nations that have bizarre attitudes in relation to human rights. This is particularly true in regard to women, thieves and anyone involved with the crime of converting Muslims to other faiths. Women wear veils for two reasons: to hide their physical features from the stares of men and to prevent the women from returning flirtatious glances. Those suspected of flirtation are subject to the same punishment that would be given to an adulterer, which is public flogging. Thieves have their hands amputated. Undercover documentaries that were aired in the fall of 2001 demonstrated horrendous punishments that had been caught on film. One woman was executed by a shot through her head for the crime of adultery. Several others received one hundred lashes each while thousands of cheering men looked on. Their crime was flirtation, as they had been observed walking with men that were not blood relatives. One hapless woman had her thumb surgically removed. Her vile deed was wearing fingernail polish. A Fundamentalist held up her severed thumb for all to see, just as he had a thief's hand moments previously. The crowd went wild with shouts of approval. In addition, at any given moment across the Muslim world, there are people being imprisoned, tortured and killed for converting to another religion or attempting to encourage others to do so.

I recently read an account of twelve young men that were charged with being traitors to Islam in Dacca, Bangladesh. Twenty thousand men and women cheered as soldiers led them into the center of a stadium's field. The soldiers bayoneted each of them in the chest and abdomen. The crowd chanted, "*Allah Akbar*", and filed down in an orderly manner to where the men lay in their death pangs. One by one, the crowd took turns stomping on the men. The men's bodies were disintegrated into pulverized masses of flesh, blood, and bones. Only a demonized religion could incite humans to act in such a barbarous manner.

To Muslims, all of the aforementioned pass as reasonable because they are supported by the sayings of Mohammed.

- Mohammed espoused spousal-abuse as a form of punishment. His admonition for correcting an uncooperative wife was to abstain from sexual relations with her and, if necessary, to beat her. *"...As to those women on whose part ye fear disloyalty and ill-conduct, Admonish them, refuse to share their beds, beat them,...*" - Quran Surah 4:34

- *"The woman and the man guilty of adultery or fornication, flog each of them with a hundred stripes; let not compassion move you in their case, in a matter prescribed by Allah, if ye believe in Allah and the Last Day; and let a party of the believers witness their punishment."* - Quran Surah 24:2
- Women are not permitted to wear wigs. Mohammed's words against wigs are likely extended to those that would use the artificial help of fingernail polish. He said, *"Don't wear false hair for Allah sends His curse upon such ladies who lengthen their hair artificially."* - Al Bukhari, Vol. 7:133
- Female Genital Mutilation (FGM) is a destructive, invasive procedure that is usually performed on girls before puberty. Part or the entire clitoris is surgically removed. This leaves them with reduced or no sexual feeling. It is a cultural practice that did not originate in Islam. However, it is practiced in some Muslim societies as a preventative measure against the temptation of girls to engage in premarital sex. Mohammed was aware of the practice, and he gave a woman advice about how it should be done. A discussion was recorded between Mohammed and Um Habibah (or Um 'Atiyyah), a woman who performed FGM on slaves. She said that she would continue the procedure, "*unless it is forbidden and you order me to stop doing it*". He replied, "*Yes, it is allowed. Come closer so I can teach you: if you cut, do not overdo it, because it brings more radiance to the face and it is*

more pleasant for the husband." - Sunan of Abu Dawud, Chapter 1888

- Under Islam convicted thieves are not given social rehabilitation during their prison terms. Their punishment puts them in need of physical rehabilitation. *"As to the thief, male or female, cut off his or her hands: A punishment, by way of example, from Allah for their crime: and Allah is exalted in power."* - Quran Surah 5:38
- Muslims do not have the human right to convert to religions of their choice. If they do, they can be punished according to the "*apostasy rule*", which states that such persons should be punished by death. Mohammed said, *"Whoever changes his religion, kill him.*" - Al Bukhari, Vol. 9:57
- Those that attempt to convert a Muslim to another faith risk severe reprisals: *"The only punishments of those who wage war against Allah and His Messenger and strive to make mischief in the land is that they should be murdered, or crucified, or their hands and their feet should be cut off on opposite sides, or they should be imprisoned."* - Quran Surah 5:33

Cruelty permitted

It is very apparent that Islam does not predispose a mindset that would motivate its adherents to initiate legislation that forbids cruel and unusual punishment. When Pakistan defeated Bangladesh in 1971, Pakistani soldiers raped two hundred fifty thousand girls and women. They could do so without shame due to the cultural absolutions available to them through Islam. Soldiers of Christianized nations would have been court-martialed and executed for this offense.

In late October of 2001, the MSNBC news channel aired a documentary that was part of the National Geographic Explorer series. It featured Afghanistan. The narrator showed, and explained convincing footage that men are incited to be pro-terrorism and anti-women by Islam. Again, the finger of guilt can be pointed at Mohammed and the clerics that emphasize selected portions of his sayings from the holy books. The spiritual power that spoke to him gave him some admirable instructions about the equitable manner in which women should be treated. However, the same spiritual entity inspired him with attitudes that negated almost all of the positive revelations that had been offered. These attitudes are totally inconsistent with Judeo-Christian attitudes toward women. They are by no means reminiscent of the injunctions that our loving Heavenly Father gave about marital relationships or the treatment of women, when the Holy Spirit inspired the Apostles that wrote the New Testament.

- It cannot be said that the Prophet did not enjoy the company of women. To the contrary, he must have because he had at least eleven wives and an unknown number of concubines. *"Anas said, 'The prophet used to visit all his wives in an hour round, during the day and night and they were eleven in number.' I asked Anas, 'Had the prophet the strength for it?' Anas replied, 'We used to say that the prophet was given the strength of thirty (men).'"* - Al Bukhari, Vol. 1:268
- Mohammed married a six-year-old girl. *"Narrated Aisha that the prophet married her when she was six years old and he consummated his marriage when she was nine years old."* - Al Bukhari, Vol. 7:64
- Allah accommodated Mohammed's sexual desires. There is a Quranic verse that encouraged Mohammed to

withhold sexual intimacy from any of his wives who fell under his disfavor. Another one revealed that Allah endorsed his marriage to his adopted son's wife. One of his wives, Aisha, responded, *"O Allah's Apostle I do not see but that your Lord hurries in pleasing you."* - Al Bukhari, Vol. 7:48

- Mohammed said things that denigrated women and would lead his followers to believe that women are mentally deficient. All of these quotes are taken from the Al Bukhari. *"After me I have not left any affliction more harmful to men than women."* (Vol. 7:33) *"I was shown the Hell-fire and that the majority of its dwellers are women."* (Vol. 1:28, 301; Vol. 2:161; Vol. 7:124) *"Bad omen is in the woman, the house and the horse."* (Vol. 7:30) Mohammed asked some women, *"Isn't the witness of a woman equal to half that of a man?"* The women said, "*Yes*". He said, *"This is because of the deficiency of the woman's mind"*. (Vol. 3:826) Mohammed to women: *"I have not seen anyone more deficient in intelligence and religion than you"*. (Vol. 2:541)

Those that are equipped with the insights presented in this chapter might be developing a new perspective on Islam. Most would hardly welcome the prospects of attending forums where Islamic fundamentalists are speaking on human rights and equal rights for women.

Chapter 5:
Mohammed's Myths

The Hadiths (the sayings and actions) of Mohammed, as recorded in the Sahih Al-Bukhari, contain many of the fanciful myths of the Prophet. I call them myths because they do not agree with biblical or scientific facts or ordinary common sense. In this chapter I will present a number of the myths that belie the notion that Mohammed received infallible inspiration from God and that he possessed a firm grasp on reality.

Mohammed's medical insights

- The key to health is a diet of camel's milk and camel's urine. *"The prophet ordered them to follow his camels, and drink their milk and urine, so they followed the camels and drank their milk and urine till their bodies became healthy."* - Al Bukhari, Vol. 7:590
- You do not need to be concerned if a fly falls into your food. Antibiotics on one wing neutralize any germs that might be on its other wing. *"If a housefly falls in the drink of any one of you, he should dip it (in the drink), for one of its wings has a disease and the other has the cure for the disease."* - Al Bukhari, Vol. 4:537
- Fever is caused by heat from hell. Mohammed said, *"Fever is from the heat of hell, so put it out (cool it) with water".* - Al Bukhari, Vol. 7:619
- The physical features of an infant are determined by which of his or her parents first experienced orgasm during its conception. If true, Islamic societies that practice FGM should be experiencing a dearth in the births of girl babies with feminine features. This stands to

reason, as women that have undergone this barbaric procedure are incapable of experiencing orgasms. In response to the questions of a woman who performed the FGM procedure, he said, "*Yes, it is allowed. Come closer so I can teach you: if you cut, do not overdo it, because it brings more radiance to the face and it is more pleasant for the husband.*" (Sunan of Abu Dawud, Chapter 1888) "*As for the child, if the man's discharge precedes the woman's discharge, the child attracts the similarity of the man, and if the woman's discharge precedes the man's, then the child attracts the similarity of the woman.*" - Al Bukhari, Vol. 5:275

- If you get urine on your clothes, you will be tortured in the after-life. "*The deceased person is being tortured in the grave not for a great thing to avoid, it is for being soiled with his urine.*" - Al Bukhari, Vol. 2:460
- Women are the blight of mankind. "*After me I have not left any affliction more harmful to men than women.*" - Al Bukhari, Vol. 7:33
- Be careful to avoid looking directly into people's eyes when speaking with them because an "*evil eye*" can be detrimental to one's well being. "*The effect of an evil eye is a fact.*" - Al Bukhari, Vol. 7:636

Mohammed's scientific discoveries

- The earth does not rotate. It is stationary because it sits on the peaks of high mountains. "*He created the heavens without any pillars that ye can see; He set on the earth mountains standing firm, lest it should shake with you; and He scattered through it beasts of all kinds. We send down rain from the sky, and produce on the earth every kind of noble creature, in pairs."* - Quran Surah 31:10

- Alexander the Great found the sun sitting in a pool of water while on one of his treks on the battlefield. *"They ask thee concerning Zul-qarnain (Alexander the Great) Say, "I will rehearse to you something of his story. Verily we established his power on earth, and we gave him the ways and the means to all ends. One (such) way he followed, until, when he reached the setting of the sun, he found it set in a spring of murky water: Near it he found a People: We said: O Zul-qarnain! (thou hast authority,) either to punish them, or to treat them with kindness."* - Quran Surah 18:83-88
- The stars are missiles that God uses to knock demons from the sky. *"The creation of these stars is for three purposes; as decoration of the sky, as missiles to hit the devils, and as signs to guide travelers."* - Al Bukhari, Vol. 4 page 282
- If a Muslim fails to awaken in time for the dawn call to prayer, it is because Satan urinated in his ears. *"Narrated Abdullah: the prophet was told that a person had kept on sleeping till morning and had not got up for the prayer. The prophet said, 'Satan urinated in his ears'."* - Al Bukhari, Vol. 2:245
- Yawning is a satanically inspired reflex. The Prophet said, *"Yawning is from Satan and if anyone of you yawns, he should check his yawning as much as possible, for if anyone of you (in the act of yawning) say: 'Ha', Satan will laugh at him."* - Al Bukhari, Vol. 4:509

Mohammed's contradictions of the Bible

- The Bible says that Cain killed Abel and that God asked him about the whereabouts of his brother. According to the Quran, Allah gave Cain instructions about how to hide the fact that he had killed his brother Abel. Supposedly, he sent a raven that demonstrated how to cover the body with dirt. *"Then Allah sent a crow who scratched the ground to show him to hide the dead body of his brother. He (the murderer) said: "Woe to me! Am I not even able to be as this crow and to hide the dead body of my brother? Then he became one of those who regretted."* - Quran Surah 5:31
- The Bible says that Noah's entire family was preserved from the flood by the ark. In the Quran Surah 11:42-43 the prophet claimed that one of Noah's sons perished in the flood.
- The Christian scriptures say that Haman lived in Persia during the reign of King Ahasuerus, the husband of Esther. Mohammed stated that Haman lived in Egypt hundreds of years previously during Moses' time. - Quran Surah 28:6
- The Bible records that Jesus was born in a manger and that He did not perform any miracles until after His temptation in the wilderness. The Quran says that Mary gave birth to Him under a palm tree and that He turned a clay bird into a living animal while He was yet a toddler. - Quran Surah 19:23, 3:49

Chapter 6: Can All Muslims Be Trusted?

All people of all religions lie occasionally, as it is a generic weakness of the human race. The Quran, like the Bible, has injunctions that forbid lying. Therefore, there are certainly some Muslims and many Christians that are conscientious enough to feel the prick of conscience if they lie to family members and others with whom they have close interpersonal relationships. However, there is strong evidence that the average Muslim would have a significantly higher inclination toward lying than most Christians. Without question, there is ample evidence that the majority of radical Muslims and the spokesmen for Islamic states are accomplished masters of deception.

Sanctioned lying

Unlike Christianity and Judaism, Islam does not simply make a provision for forgiveness if one tells a lie; it actually encourages lying in certain situations. This is evident in both the Quran and the Hadith. The latter is a collection of Mohammed's sayings and deeds according to his wives, relatives, and companions. Next to the Quran, it is the most important part of Islamic law. In the Hadith, Mohammed was quoted as saying, *"The sons of Adam are accountable for all lies with the exception of those spoken to reconcile two men that are quarreling, for a man to appease his wife, and in war, because war necessitates deception."* This is what often makes life such a nightmare for non-Muslim women that marry Muslim men. Without the pangs of conscience, men are licensed to appease their wives with promises which they have no intention of keeping. In addition, within Islam there is the principle of "*Al Takeyya*". The term means, "*the prevention*".

This principle permits Muslims to lie at their discretion whenever they interpret that it is expedient for the influence of Islam or their personal welfare. They justify lying by using the following verse as a springboard for expanded applications of Al Takeyya. *"Let not the believers take the disbelievers for friends rather than believers. And whoever does this has no connection with Allah unless it is done to guard (Takeyya) yourselves against them, guarding carefully. And Allah cautions you against His retribution. And to Allah is the eventual coming."* (Quran 3:27) The principle of Al Takeyya is precisely what makes negotiations with Islamic statesmen such a frustrating endeavor for the naïve diplomats of Christianized nations. It is imperative that diplomatic envoys learn that when dealing with Muslims, what Muslim statesmen say is not the issue. The real issue is, what do they mean and actually intend to do in their hearts.

There is a spiritual reason that prevents many of the aforementioned from experiencing the pangs of conscience as they routinely lie when dealing with non-Muslims. It is permissible for them to lie because Mohammed's Quranic revelations, unlike God's revealed will in the Bible, permits lying if it can be perceived as an effort to extend the influence of Islam.

Father of lies

On one occasion Jesus accused the Pharisees of ancient Judaism of being the sons of the father of lies. He said, *"You are of your father the devil, and the desires of your father you want to do. He was a murderer from the beginning, and does not stand in the truth, because there is no truth in him. When he speaks a lie, he speaks from his own resources, for he is a liar and the father of it"* (John 8:44). If the Son of God could say this of the radical zealots of the Mosaic Laws that were authored by His Heavenly

Father, it is likely that lying is even more endemic among those that represent a religion that is ridden with confusion and contradictions. I will pose a number of spiritual and historical points that may be worth pondering.

Islam's Allah

We must begin with Mohammed's Allah. Who or what was the spiritual entity that gave the revelations found in the Quran and the Hadith to Mohammed? It is certain that it was not the Divine Personage that is described in the Christian English Bible, or its Arabic version, as God or "*Allah*". The holy books of Islam depict Mohammed's Allah with a character and attributes that are incompatible with those of the Loving God (Allah) of the Bible. To demonstrate this I will give a brief summary of Christianity 101. The truths that I am offering are well understood by any Christian that has been confirmed as a Catholic or been exposed to preaching from the Bible. Teachings and some quotations from the Islamic holy books will follow this summary. These holy books contain the sayings and deeds of Mohammed that he alleged were inspired directly by Allah. The Prophet claimed that the Angel Gabriel, that was supposedly also the Holy Spirit, initially contacted him and informed him that Allah would be speaking to him about the true faith. The stark contrast between Christianity and Islam will alert the reader's discernment to the reality that the spiritual power that claimed to be Allah and the God of Christianity, the true Allah, are not the same. This will call for the need to explain just what type of spiritual entity Mohammed might have been encountering over the twenty-two years of his revelations. The reader will see that Muslims attach attributes to Allah that are not indicative of the one true God of Christianity and the Bible.

Christianity 101

God, the true Allah, is the Creator of all things. He does not change and He is not the author of confusion but rather of peace. If He makes a promise, He swears by the value of His own name that He will keep it. The Lord God swears by Himself, the "*I Am*". He does not swear by anything that He has created because He is greater than anything that He has created. The Bible says that God is "*one*", yet it also speaks of the Godhead. The members of the Godhead are called the *Trinity* because the *Three* are "*one*" in their unity. As three uniquely distinct Persons - Father, Son and Holy Spirit - they flow in perfectly harmonious agreement. In the Bible the term "*one*" speaks of unity as well as number. For instance, husband and wife are described as "*one flesh*", though they are two separate persons of different sexes and functions within the marriage. The Apostle Paul said that anyone that was a Christian was "*one*" with Christ. It is obvious that this means unity as opposed to a numerical value because at this moment there are well over a billion Christians living on the planet. When the prophet John baptized Christ, he heard the Father speaking from heaven and he saw the Holy Spirit coming upon Jesus like a dove (Matt. 3:16-17). If God the Father, God the Son, and God the Holy Spirit were actually a singular divine person, it would indicate that Jesus was performing simultaneously as a ventriloquist and an illusionist.

The obedient Son

The Father sent the Son to earth to live a life of complete obedience to the Laws of Moses, which mankind could not keep faithfully. Then Jesus died on the cross and was physically resurrected by the Holy Spirit from the dead. In His death and resurrection, He provided a way for men to receive credit for being completely righteous in God's sight without being obligated to obey each of His laws to the letter. Those that repent and believe that God raised Jesus from the dead are credited with the righteousness of Jesus. Anyone that does this is guaranteed heaven at death. Jesus said that no man that the Father had given Him could be plucked out of His hand. We are not to embrace another Gospel even if it is a revelation from an angelic being. God makes few demands on the redeemed that are absolutes. Two of them are that we must love others as Christ did and forgive others as He did. In heaven there will be no need for sexual intimacy because the glory of our companionship with God will overshadow the need for it. Anyone that persists in an unrepentant lifestyle involving lying, idolatry, or deviate sexual behavior cannot inherit the Kingdom of God.

Islam is very different

- The Quran reveals that the Muslim Allah is lower than his creation. Twenty-four times in the Quran, Allah swears by something other than himself: the angels, the winds, a mountain, a star, the sky, the sun and so on. It is like going to court as a witness and instead of swearing on the Bible or even the Quran; you would swear to tell the truth based on the authority of, say, a goldfish or a housefly.
- The true Allah, the God of Christians, is the Supreme Ruler over all things. God is love, but He cannot be manipulated by anything or anyone in His creation. Mohammed's Allah has every appearance of being the Prophet's pawn. He conveniently intervened to accommodate Mohammed's sexual desires, to support

his opinions and to justify his actions whenever he was in trouble.

- The Islamic Allah could not be one and the same as the God of Abraham, Isaac and Jacob because he is subject to change and vacillation in his opinions. *"Our revelations we abrogate or cause to be forgotten, we substitute (with) something better or similar. Knowest thou not that God (Allah) hath power over all things."* - Quran Surah 2:106
- The Holy Spirit did not inspire the Quran, as it contains too many confusing contradictions. In January of 1999 the Atlantic Monthly magazine began a three-part series on the Quran. It was written by Toby Lester and entitled "*What is the Koran?*" In the third installment an authority on Islam was quoted as saying: *"Gerd-R Puin speaks with disdain about the traditional willingness, on the part of Muslim and Western scholars, to accept the conventional understanding of the Koran. 'The Koran claims for itself that it is "mubeen", or clear'. He says, 'But if you look at it, you will notice that every fifth sentence or so simply doesn't make sense. Many Muslims -- and Orientalists -- will tell you otherwise, of course, but the fact is that a fifth of the Quranic text is just incomprehensible. This is what has caused the traditional anxiety regarding translation. If the Koran is not comprehensible -- if it can't even be understood in Arabic -- then it's not translatable. People fear that. And since the Koran claims repeatedly to be clear but obviously is not -- as even speakers of Arabic will tell you -- there is a contradiction. Something else must be going on.'"*

- . This article provides an excellent explanation for what would otherwise be an enigma to those that attempt to study various translations of the Quran. The student soon discovers that there is a significant difference in the way various translators translate the same texts. This can be confusing unless one understands several things. The fact that the Quran has large portions that are incomprehensible even in Arabic leaves much to the discretion of individual translators. Many of them desire to present Islam in a favorable light as a religion of peace. These often modify the Quranic texts in a manner that they believe will make their faith appear less primitive, hostile and barbarous.
- Islam's Allah could not be the same as the God of Christians because he disclaimed membership in the Trinity and that Christ was God. *"They do blaspheme who say Allah is one of three in a Trinity, for there is no god except One Allah."* (Quran Surah 5:73) *"In blasphemy indeed are those that say that Allah (God) is Christ the son of Mary. Say: who then hath the least power against Allah if His will were to destroy Christ the son of Mary, his mother, and all - everyone that is on earth? For to Allah belongeth the dominion of the heavens and the earth, and all that is in between... For Allah hath power over all things."* - Quran Surah 5:17
- Mohammed's Allah said that Jesus did not die by crucifixion. *"That they said (in boast), we killed Christ Jesus, the Son of Mary. But, they killed him not, nor crucified him."* - Quran Surah 4:157
- According to some Muslim theologians, the texts below indicate that Islamic heaven is a place where male

Muslims will have sex orgies with beautiful women and with beautiful young boys. The two Arabic words that are used for boys (or youths) are *Wildan* and *Gholman*, which mean *eternally young beautiful boys or young men. "As to the righteous, they will be in gardens and in happiness (to them will be said:) Eat and drink ye, with profit and health, because of your (good) deeds." "They will recline (with ease) on thrones (of dignity) arranged in ranks; and we shall join (marry) them to companions with beautiful big and lustrous eyes... And we shall bestow on them, of fruit and meat, anything they desire. They shall there exchange, one another, a cup free of frivolity, free of all taint of ill. Round about them youths (handsome) as pearls well-guarded."* - Quran Surah 52:17, 19, 20 & 22-24.

- An article on Faith Freedom's website clarifies the reality that homosexual pedophilia is acceptable within Islam. The following is an abbreviation of a journalist's observations. He was invited to attend a wedding in the United Arab Emirates where, to his surprise, a sheikh was marrying an eleven-year-old boy. Someone felt that an explanation was in order. The guests were told that it was important that a prominent sheikh have a few boys in his harem. To validate that this was acceptable, he recited two verses from the Quran. *"And there shall wait on them young boys of their own, as fair as virgin pearl."* (52:24) *"They shall be attended by boys graced with eternal youth who to the beholders eyes will seem like sprinkle pearls."* (76:19). His report further stated that an Egyptian court had recently prosecuted thirty young homosexuals, as homosexuality is prohibited in

Islam. A summarization of his thoughts could go along this line: *"One wonders, if homosexuality is prohibited, then why does Allah promise that men that were good Muslims while alive, will have young boys as sex partners in Paradise? It must be that in instances like the Emirate sheikh's intended pedophilic sex with his male child bride it is not considered to be homosexuality. It is permissible in that it is merely pedophilia. If two mutually consenting men have sex, it is the sinful crime of homosexuality."*

- A spiritual entity representing himself to be the Holy Spirit, as well as the angel Gabriel, gave Mohammed the "*true religion*" that was to replace Judaism and Christianity. According to the Bible, the Holy Spirit is a member of the Godhead, and angels are merely God-created spiritual beings. *"Say the Holy Spirit (the Angel Gabriel) has brought the revelation (the Quran) from thy Lord in Truth."* (Quran Surah 16:102) *"Fight People of the Book (Christians and Jews), who do not accept the religion of the truth (Islam), until they pay tribute (penalty tax) by hand, being inferior."* - Quran Surah 9:29
- Mohammed taught that people in heaven could be sent to hell because of the actions of those that are still living on earth. Not even the Prophet had the assurance of eternity in heaven. *"You praised this, so Paradise has been affirmed to him, and you spoke badly of this, so hell has been affirmed to him. You people are Allah's witnesses on earth."* (Al Bukhari, Vol. 2:448) *"By Allah, though I am the apostle of Allah, yet I do not*

know what Allah will do to me." - Al Bukhari, Vol. 5:266

- Unlike the God of Christianity, the spiritual force that inspired Mohammed did not insist that people practice loving forgiveness one with another. *"If anyone transgress the prohibition against you, transgress likewise against him."* - Quran Surah 2:194

Mohammed's Allah was not divine

The aforementioned teachings of Islam give strong evidence that the Islamic Allah is not identical to the God of the Bible. What then was he? The apostle Paul warned Christians that Satan could transform into an angel of light. He also said that he was concerned about those who would come preaching under the inspiration of a spirit that was *different* from the Holy Spirit, that would declare a *different* Gospel, that would feature *another* Christ (anointed one of God). His concern was that many would be deceived into departing from authentic faith in Christ by listening to the doctrines of demons that were based on lies (2 Cor. 11:1-4, 14 & 1 Tim 4:1-2). All of this describes the events that spawned Islam. An angel of light ("*light*" is a synonym for "*revelation*") came to Mohammed and said that he was both Gabriel and the Holy Spirit. This mixture definitely makes this being of an entirely *different* spiritual species than the divine, eternal Holy Spirit of God. Mohammed was deceived into believing that he was superior in anointing to Christ. This would infer a *different* Christ or anointed one. The Prophet then began to proclaim the demonic doctrinal lie that he had a religion that was "*better news*" for mankind than the Gospel of Jesus. (The word *Gospel* means *good news*.) So he was surely preaching a *different* Gospel. Therefore, the spiritual entity that gave revelations to

Mohammed was at best a lying, deceiving spirit and at worst Satan, the father of lies, representing himself to be an angel of light.

The reason that we cannot trust the commitments that are made in negotiations with the representatives of radical Muslim nations is because they adhere to a religion that is built on lies. A corrupt tree cannot bring forth good fruit. A religion that is polluted by deceptions from the father of lies cannot inspire its zealots to be truthful when dealing with their enemies. There is resplendent evidence that the sayings and attitudes of Mohammed continually play a major role in producing an absence of truthfulness from Islamic authorities when they are in negotiations with Non-Muslims.

- Mohammed taught that the value of a Muslim's life was greater than that of a non-Muslim. If people do not value one's life, it is foolish to presume that they would put a high value on telling one the truth and keeping their commitments. *"No Muslim should be killed for killing a kafir (infidel or non-Muslim)."* - Al Bukhari, Vol. 9:50
- Muslims do not believe that they are accountable for spontaneous promises. When they are dealing with non-Muslims, it is perfectly acceptable to tell them what is expeditious in a given situation, even if it does not express the true intentions of their hearts. *"God will not call you to account for thoughtlessness in your oaths, but for the intention in your hearts; and He is Oft-forgiving, Most Forbearing."* - Quran Surah 2:225
- The PLO perpetually tells governmental envoys and news correspondents of democratic nations that they want a peace agreement with Israel. While it is true that they want an agreement, it is not true that they really want

peace. Behind the scenes they plot ways to disrupt agreements and make it appear that Israel is the villain. The PLO TV network televises news reports that applaud terrorism as the acts of heroic freedom fighters and feature the speeches of PLO spokesmen that generate more hostilities.

- Iraq's ambassadors to various democratic nations constantly affirmed that their nation did not possess and had never used biological weapons. Several months later, thousands of Kurds perished by the effects of biological warfare in Northern Iraq.
- During the War on Iraq, Hussein's Minister of Information demonstrated the Islamic propensity to lie without conscience. He claimed that the Coalition's forces were nowhere near Baghdad. The truth is, they were taking showers in Hussein's palace several blocks from the site where he was being interviewed.
- Libya claimed that it knew nothing about the terrorist bombing of a Pan Am airliner over Scotland. The terrorists that had perpetrated the crime were later traced to Libya.
- Representatives of the coalition against terrorism are finally waking up to the fact that radical Muslims cannot be trusted. In this regard during October of 2001, televised news reports constantly repeated a statement made by the American Secretary of Defense, Donald Rumsfeld. He said, "*We are learning that the Taliban officials of Afghanistan are accomplished liars*".

Muslims butcher Muslims

Observations that punctuate the absurdity of the façade that Islam is a peaceful religion are almost endless. If Israel or the Coalition against international terrorism happens to accidentally harm civilians, the Muslim world riots in protest. There have been no international Muslim protests over the numerous incidences in which Muslim terrorists purposely maimed and killed citizens of free societies. Muslim communities around the globe take it in stride when factions within Islam commit genocide against one another in Jordan, Syria, Afghanistan, Egypt, Algeria, and Tunisia. In 1970, King Hussein of Jordan got wind that the Palestinians were going to attempt to take a portion of Jordan as their homeland. In a military campaign that is now called "*Black September*", he sent troops into the refugee camps of Southern Jordan and Lebanon. It is estimated that as many as four thousand Palestinians perished in the assaults. The global Muslim community did not riot in protests of this atrocity against their displaced brethren.

During the month of February of 1982 it became apparent that Islamic extremists headquartered in Hama, Syria were mounting an effort to make Syria an Islamic-governed state. President Hafez al-Assad took decisively brutal action. He bombarded the city with artillery and then had it bulldozed into the appearance of a giant parking lot. Amnesty International estimates that from ten thousand to twenty-five thousand civilians were slaughtered in the siege. There were no reports of the Muslims in other nations crying out that this was a grievous injustice against innocent civilians. It is interesting to note that when natural disasters strike Muslim countries, one rarely sees mercy missions initiated from fellow Muslim nations rushing to their aid. There are no occurrences of relief efforts coming from Islamic societies when disasters strike non-Muslim countries. Whenever and wherever disasters occur, the world can depend upon the financial resources and the relief efforts of nations that are built on Judeo-Christian values. Relief is dispersed to all, regardless of their nationality or religion. It is apparent that Islam is as inept at fostering merciful compassion as it is in accomplishing harmonious co-existence among people of diverse faiths.

If what has been presented in this book is only a partially accurate assessment, you know the answer to the question that titles this last chapter. Can all Muslims be trusted? No! As a religion, Islam simply does not program its adherents to understand and reflect all of the positive values that are treasured by Christians, Jews and those of numerous other spiritual disciplines. I will use an analogy based upon computer hard-drives to bring understanding as to why it is next to impossible for Westerners to have successful negotiations with Islamic authorities. The psyches of the citizens of Christian nations and those of Muslim states are very much like the hard-drives of computers. The citizens of the respective nations will respond to situations based upon the spiritual and social data that has been programmed into their hard-drives. The inner programming of people with Christian values and those with Muslim programming is entirely different. In relation to peace we have vastly diverse programming as to what it entails. A generalization would offer the following: For Westerners peace is the absence of aggression in an environment where people of different nationalities can harmoniously pursue happiness. For Islamic nations, peace is all the citizens of a nation endeavoring to obey the dictates of Mohammed in an environment where the presence of aggression is a legitimate means to achieve eventual harmonious compliance. The representatives of Christian societies will not be successful in making productive, long-term, peace agreements with Muslims until their inner hard-drives have been programmed with data that will help them process the innuendoes of Islamic negotiators.

Unreliable allies

In addition, the differences in inner programming are the specific reasons that Islamic controlled nations are not reliable allies for Westernized democracies. There is overwhelming evidence that Muslim leaders affirm friendship, but inevitably demonstrate betrayal. Saudi Arabia claims to be a faithful ally and simultaneously blatantly awards financial grants to the families of homicide-bombers that slaughter Israeli citizens. Intelligence reports that came out in 2003 implied that members of the Saudi government had ties to the 9/11 terrorists. Pakistan vows support in the War on Terrorism and took our millions of dollars to supposedly assist them in their battle. However, it is very clear that they are dragging in their feet in seeking out Osama Bin Baden and that segments of their intelligence community are actually his cohorts. Egypt receives billions in foreign aid from America and their population rejoices when Islamic terrorists score successes against us. Turkey has been the most cooperative among the bunch, yet they would not allow us to launch attacks on Hussein's forces in the War on Iraq from within their borders. We even give millions to Syria. It is a refuge for terrorists and members of Hussein's deposed government. There are indications that Syria aided Iraq by allowing them to hide weapons of mass destruction in their territory. All Western diplomats must come to understand that if the leaders of nations are Islamic, the Al Takeyya principle permits them to knowingly lie and transgress in agreements with infidels.

Erroneous perspectives

America, Great Britain, Germany, France and other European nations all have their respective programs to aid Islamic states. The naïve hope is that somehow such funding will charm them into behaving and playing fair. Two erroneous perspectives spawn these give-away programs. The first is that ignorance feeds terrorism and that education is the cure. This is belied by several facts. The leaders of the various Islamic terrorist organizations are not uneducated. Most of them were educated in Western countries. The foot soldiers that commit the acts of terrorism are better educated than most of the populations of the nations that send aid to Islamic states. Those that plant the bombs speak the languages of the respective nations wherein they perpetrate their mayhem. Few of their innocent victims speak any of the Middle-Eastern dialects. In addition, the Quran is written in an antiquated, formal style of Arabic. Only the educated can read it and less than 30% of the world's Muslims speak any form of Arabic as their native tongue. The implications are clear. It is the educated that read, proliferate, and enact Mohammed's and the Quran's hostile messages.

The second erroneous perspective is that poverty causes terrorism. This premise is ludicrous in that other impoverished groups do not routinely resort to terror to rectify their situations. Even if it happened to be a major contributing factor, pitifully few of the billions of dollars that free societies offer are actually used to alleviate the poverty of the general populations of Islamic nations. PLO chairman, Yassur Arafat, used millions to train terrorists, buy arms, and to make himself a multi-millionaire. The billions that Iraq collected from the West in the "oil for food program" did little for its starving masses. Hussein siphoned significant portions of the funds in a similar manner as Arafat. It has been discovered that the leftover funds from his building of palaces and buying weapons are now being used to finance terrorism against the Coalition's troops in post-war Iraq.

Recommendations

I will close this chapter with some guidelines as to how to respond to the contents of this book and then we will proceed to the final two important chapters.

- All Western democracies should be encouraged to cease and desist from giving foreign aid to Islamic states that harbor terrorists. Any aid that is given should be distributed onsite by representatives of the providing nations. The UN and other international agencies cannot be trusted to administer such funds for the intended purposes efficiently.
- I know that clever men, anointed by the Holy Spirit for the task, authored our Bill of Rights and its Amendments to our Constitution. We now need keen legislative minds to lobby creative suggestions for updating the amendments. Our current Congressional representatives can be inspired to craft legislation that will protect us from our foes without violating the spirit of the Constitution. Even if it might ultimately require a Constitutional Convention, concerned Americans must begin to voice the necessity of this to their representatives.
- Resist any legislation that would empower tax-exempt religious organizations with increased abilities for political influence. The Conservative Christian Right recently lobbied for laws that would permit them to use larger percentages of their funds for political purposes. This ploy is satanically deceptive. It equally empowers Islam to use its vast resources to sway our politicians and to assert its agenda for religious dominance from mosques.
- Our government would serve us well by enacting laws that would discourage excessive foreign funding for religious

groups within the United States. The Saudis and other oil-producing Islamic states are now funding our Islamization under the guise of charity to US-based Muslim institutions. In effect, our petrodollars are financing the demise of our way of life. This could be discouraged by a ruling that would dictate that 50% of such gifts be conscripted by our government and that only 50% be made available to the intended charities. A portion of the government's collected fees could help finance our war on terror and homeland security. The remaining portion could be used to reimburse Americans that have been paying excessive prices at the gas pump for years.

- We should call for a restriction on the number of visas granted to Islamic foreign nationals each year. We must demand that the Department of Homeland Security closely monitor those that currently hold educational and business visas. Those that are in visa violation should be instantly deported.
- Organize petitions that support legislation that will help detect and deter potential terrorists. This could include: The right of police to investigate Mosques that are suspect of aiding and abetting terrorism; the detention and rapid deportation of foreign nationals that are suspected of inciting or financially supporting acts of aggression toward your nation; stopping the issuing of student and work visas to individuals from Islamic states that are known to support terrorism; the right of government officials to investigate the current activities of foreign nationals that have secured work or student visas in the past five years; and finally by insisting that public transportation facility security check points be manned by

individuals that are directly accountable to your nation's government.

- According to many experts on international terrorism, Saudi Arabia is the major culprit for the funding of Islamic terrorists. The concerned citizens of endangered countries should demand that their respective United Nations ambassadors put pressure on Saudi Arabia to discontinue its support of terrorist organizations.
- The best way to win Muslims to Jesus is through friendship evangelism. This means that any efforts to convert them must be preceded by demonstrations that you truly value them as individuals and genuinely care for the welfare of their families. During this period it is strategic that they see that God answers your prayers and that your faith in Christ makes you a loving, hospitable, courteous and productive person. In this regard it is helpful that you pray for their needs and those of their family while in their presence. Do not offer mini-sermons as you pray for them. Simply pray for specific needs in the name of Jesus and then follow up with inquiries about how things are going. The signal that it is time to share the gospel message is an occasion when they initiate questions about your faith. It is good to open with some type of gentle statement that defines why people from other nations desire to immigrate to Christianized nations. The reason being, the Christian faith nurtured the prosperity and blessings of God that make those nations attractive. Statements of this nature are posed to get Muslims pondering why Islam has not brought similar blessings to their homelands. To continue beyond this point you will need to be familiar with all of the Quranic

verses that speak about Jesus. This will enable you to flow from areas where Islam and Christianity are in agreement into areas where they differ. You will need to be equipped to present biblically sound, cohesive logic for your beliefs in the trinity, the divinity of Christ and His sacrificial death and physical resurrection. You should also be prepared to offer the differences between the Christian concepts of forgiveness, freedom from stringent requirements to conform to religious laws, eternal security and heaven, and those of Islam. Finally, do not look for a single conversation to be the impetus to convert them. When Muslims are won to Jesus, it is normally the fruit of numerous relaxed and friendly conversations.

- Exercise love and respect towards members of your nation's Muslim communities. Do not harass them or perpetrate hate crimes against their homes, businesses or Mosques. To do so will simply add to the potential to fan the flames justifying terrorism. In addition, hate crimes are un-Christian and illegal. They are a violation of the national civil rights laws of most democratic nations. If you know of anyone that is voicing threats of such crimes, report it to the proper police agencies.

If the contents of this book have resonated within you, pass it out to your friends, business associates, and clergymen. Mail copies to your governmental representatives. Engage in discussions with others that will enlighten them about the facade that cloaks the Muslim masquerade.

Chapter 7:
Muslim Friend, Wake Up

A call for Muslims to reevaluate Islam
as they enter the Twenty-first Century

Muslims have genuine capacities for love, compassion, and noble achievements. The majority of those that I know personally are affable, productive members of society. Like all people, they also carry the potential for counterproductive, destructive behaviors. There is something, however, that Muslims have that has for centuries caused many to live beneath their abilities. It is currently causing them embarrassment within the global community. The culprit is their faithful allegiance with Islam's demands that all Muslims comply with its eccentricities.

All religions have embarrassing islands of history. Commonly, most have obscure, antiquated, doctrinal elements that are not compatible with contemporary sensitivities. None are exempt from fringe radicals that find purpose and identity by expressing these bizarre elements. Islam, however, stands alone in its ability to incite the masses. Its basic doctrines compel its fundamentalists to enact extremist policies. The moderates comply through their silence. They are silent because they know that the fundamentalists accurately depict what Islam teaches. The end result is that Islam continues to espouse principles that defy the expectations of what most civil people would perceive as acceptable behavior. The purpose of this article is to challenge Muslims to assess what Islam has produced in societies heretofore. Hopefully, this will persuade them to reevaluate its ability to empower them for the Twenty-first Century.

Repetitive behavior + expecting different results = Insanity

Most Muslims, like most people that are labeled as Jews and Christians, did not purposely choose their religious label. The label bestowed on them was a matter of birth rather than a personal decision of conscience. The distinction is, those labeled as Muslims, in spite of their personal aspirations, are weighted with a religious system that has failed to bless cultures. On the other hand, regardless of their personal attributes, those labeled as Jews and Christians have been carried along by the blessings inherent within Judeo-Christian cultures. This is verified by the national economic and educational statistics of the World Almanac. A comparison of statistical information on Islamic-controlled nations and Western democracies indicates acute disparities between the two.

This begs certain questions amongst thinking people. Are people that carry certain religious labels innately more intelligent than others? Are they born with abilities for creative business ventures and technological advances that surpass those of others? Of course, the answer to both of these questions is, No. The basic difference between the three people-groups in question is spiritual programming. None is genetically predisposed to be more creative and progressive than the other. Spiritual surgery removing the teachings of Mohammed from the hearts and minds of the people of Muslim countries would be beneficial. Within a relatively short period it would put them on an even plain with other nations. Reason should caution people from continuing with belief systems that have failed to produce tangible blessings for the people of nations that would otherwise be blessed.

The tale of two nations

In short, you can tell the value of a religion by observing the plight of nations that have lived under its influence for an extended period. If a religion has merit, it will inspire creativity from those that adhere to it. South Korea was predominantly Buddhist prior to its war with Communist North Korea in 1950. Christian nations defended South Korea, and subsequently the majority of its citizens have embraced Christianity as their religion of choice. Even though its economy was devastated by the war, it has risen from the ash heap and now has a gross national product (GNP) that dwarfs those of the oil rich Islamic-controlled nations. Christianized South Korea's GNP for 2001 was $764.8 billion. Its per capita income was $16,100; infant mortality rate 7.6/1000; literacy rate 98%; and its exports were electronic and electrical equipment, machinery, steel, automobiles, ships, textiles, clothing, footwear and fish.

Saudi Arabia should be the crown of Islam, as it was its birthplace in the Seventh Century. Keep in mind that Saudi Arabia's Islam claims to be superior to all other religions. These are the statistics that the "*true religion*" spawned for 2000: GNP $232 billion; per capita income $10,500; infant mortality rate 49.6/1000; literacy rate 63%; and its sole exports were petroleum and petroleum products. Considering that their clerics claim that the faithful will be blessed, this is not an impressive showing for 1,300 years of multiple daily prayers to a deity. The fact is, the royal family of Saudi Arabia would be riding on camels, rather than in air-conditioned Mercedes, if it were not for the oil drilling technology of Christian nations. Wherever Islam is the primary focus of a government, the majority of its citizens languish in an abased existence. If those same people emigrate to a democratic society, where the pursuit of happiness is primary and their degree of religious expression is optional, they are apt to flourish.

Economic progress frustrated

Whenever the value of Islam is brought into question, Muslims remind those making inquiries of its "*Golden age*". During this period, from 700 through 1200AD, Europe was in the Dark Ages. The Middle East and Asian nations that had been conquered by Islamic Jihad (holy war or struggle) led the world as they continued to make advances in the disciplines of literature, science, and math. However, there was a curious cessation of their leadership after the Eleventh Century. In contrast, progress was restored in Christianized nations during the Renaissance and continued through the Industrial Revolution into the high-tech achievements of the current era.

Islamic countries were left sitting in the sand. One would be hard pressed to cite a single original medical, industrial, or technological innovation that has come forth from an Islamic-governed nation without the support of Western influence and education. During the past five hundred years Islamic nations have not produced one contribution to science, technology or industry in a stand-alone manner. There are no innovative products for sale in the world's markets that were invented and produced by Muslims in Islamic-controlled nations. Students from the global community are not lined up to apprehend visas to study at the universities of Saudi Arabia and Afghanistan. The foreign embassies of Christian countries are flooded with visa applications from Muslims that are seeking opportunities to live in the fertile environments that are built on Judeo-Christian values. If Heaven's approval has been bestowed on Mohammed's doctrines, it would seem that we would see people from Christian nations flocking to get work and educational visas in Islamic states.

What caused the cessation of academic progress in the nations that were conquered by Islam? Did some DNA mutation kick in that caused people's intelligence to be altered? This could not be the case because many of the same nationalities prove to be brilliant in settings that are founded on principles other than interpretations of Mohammed's teachings. The Jews come from the same Abrahamic genetic pool, and their scientists and intellectuals have been awarded one hundred and thirty-nine Nobel prizes. There have been only nine Islamic recipients, and most of them were privileged with educations in Western democracies. The finger of guilt points toward the Muslim religion and the teachings of its clerics. The cessation of innovation was caused by the rule of Islam from 700 through 1200AD. It took five hundred years for it to finally take hold and totally stifle the progress of the nations that were under its influence.

America, the great Satan

Islamic supporters have a repertoire of influences to blame for the lack of progress in Islamic states. America is called the "*Great Satan*". Clerics espouse that if it were not for our evil influence, their citizens would be flowing in freedom, prosperity, and health. How soon they forget that the wealth that their leaders squander in lavish lifestyles and the medical advances that save their citizens from epidemics were birthed in Westernized democracies.

Others assert that regional conflicts and harsh environments are the culprits. Interestingly, there are other nations that have experienced the same and risen above the adversities. This will be exampled by a comparison of the statistics on Islam-controlled Iran, predominantly Lutheran Iceland, and Israel.

- Iran's stats for 2000: arable land 10%; per capita income $6,300; infant mortality rate 28.1/1000; literacy rate 79%.
- Iceland's stats for 2000: arable land 0%; per capita income $24,800; infant mortality rate 3.5/1000; literacy rate 100%.
- Israel's stats for 2000: arable land 17%; per capita income $18,900; infant mortality rate 7.5/1000; literacy rate 96%.

The statistics that have been provided thus far in this article should provoke thinking readers to ponder the possibility that there is something grossly amiss with Islam. Basic logic dictates that the faithful should be able to overcome any real or imagined satanic obstacles, if Allah is all-powerful and Islam is indeed a superior religion. To the contrary, Muslim-controlled regimes that demand that their citizens pray five times daily, obey the Quran, follow the dictates of their imams, fast the forty days of Ramadan, and make pilgrimages to Mecca have proved impotent in bringing reasonable prosperity to the masses within their societies.

Religion in the mix

It is Islamic countries, not Christianized nations that insert the spiritual dimension into every equation. The Muslims of Islamic states are usually far more zealous for the agendas of their clergymen than the nominal Christian populations of Western countries are for those espoused by their pastors. Westernized democracies that have Christianity as a prevalent religion do not call for the citizens of fellow nations to join them in holy wars against other nations. This has not occurred since the shameful period of the Crusades nine hundred years ago. During the ensuing years Christendom has undergone a major reformation. It no longer has Church-State governments. Calls to war are issued on the basis of mutual self-defense and to facilitate freedom for politically oppressed people. In isolated instances the leader of a Westernized nation might express his personal faith when his troops go to war. However, the secular compositions of genuinely free democracies prevent them from calling for war in the name of a particular faith a matter of national policy.

Islam has never had a reformation. Its leaders are following the examples of Mohammed and the early caliphs of Islam to this very day. Everything is done in the name of Allah and for the cause of Islam. All the while, these efforts belie all evidences of Heavenly support. The Jews of Israel continue to prevail regardless of the multi-national Islamic decrees calling for their extinction in the name of Allah. Saddam Hussein declared that Allah would give Iraq the victory over the infidels in 1991. His boast was that his God would give them success in what would be the Mother of all battles. Less than one hundred hours later, it proved to be the Mother of all retreats.

In the war for Iraq's freedom of 2003, Saddam's Minister of Information constantly swore, by Allah, that soldiers and peasants on the borders of Iraq were slaughtering Coalition forces. After twenty-five days of armed conflict, he was nowhere to be found, and Iraqi Muslims were kissing the hands of the infidels that liberated them. It was reported that many Iraqis were laying the blame for their culture's demise at the feet of the parties whom they believed to be responsible. These citizens physically beat and stoned the spiritual leaders that had assured them of victory. The contemporary generation of Iranians is also getting the picture. Televised documentaries on Iran that were filmed in secret have revealed some interesting facts. Those interviewed, between twenty and thirty years of age, reported that the vast majority of their contemporaries wanted to throw off the limitations of Islam and embrace Western values.

Islam vs. Judeo-Christian values

Muslims need to evaluate whether Islam will enhance their journey into the Twenty-first Century or continue to be excess baggage. The following contrasts Islam's performance versus that of nations founded on Judeo-Christian ethics. The nations and people of the latter do not make a habit of using religious precepts to rationalize unacceptable behavior. The motivations for their behavior are founded upon their desires to make meaningful contributions for the welfare of the community of mankind. Undoubtedly, these same noble aspirations reside in the hearts of many Muslims. Unfortunately, the fruition of these hopes often becomes bogged in a mire of spiritual prohibitions and technicalities. Each of the following comparisons points out unacceptable practices for which there are precedents in Islam's history and holy books. I challenge any that question the validity of what is stated to explore these two websites:

http://www.islamreview.com

http://main.faithfreedom.org

These provide Quranic and Hadith references, along with testimonies of ex-Muslims, who support what I have stated.

Cruel gender bias

Many Islamic states deny females the right to vote and equal opportunities for higher education. The policies of the majority of them demand that women wear full body *burkas*, or at least a head covering, while in public, regardless of whether or not they are Muslims. An ex-Muslim Iranian woman has a letter posted on the Faith Freedom website. This is the gist of her alarming testimony. In Iran any woman that rejects the principle of *Hijab* (head coverings) is considered an apostate. Under Islamic law the punishment for an apostate is death. Girls condemned to death may not undergo the sentence as long as they are virgins. Thus they are systematically raped before the sentence is executed. According to the clerics, the only way to prevent a virgin from going to heaven is to take her virginity. Apostates, they declare, don't deserve heaven so they are raped to insure that they will go to hell.

One of the most horrifying aspects of Islam is that it rationalizes what we would term as nothing less than pedophilic rape. A high value is placed on wives coming to the marriage bed as virgins. To insure chastity, girls are often given in marriage between the ages of nine and eleven. The moment the girls reach puberty their husbands engage in sexual intercourse with them. The men are often thirty years senior to their little wives. For these hapless children their first sexual experiences amount to frightening rapes. – *In westernized cultures women have equal rights with men. No civil authority has the right to enforce religious regulations. Anyone that sexually abuses a minor would be prosecuted to the full extent of the law.*

Human rights infractions

Statistics indicate that Muslims perpetrate a disproportionate number of human rights infractions to that of any other single religious group. Arab nations import disadvantaged boys, aged four to six, to be jockeys for camel races. The children are fed meagerly to keep them light in weight. Many are seriously injured, and some have been trampled to death. Sudan, Mauritania, and Kuwait actively engage in slavery. It is not unusual for convicted thieves to have limbs surgically removed. Women charged with adultery are stoned to death or receive a gun shot to the temple. Enactments of these punishments have been verified by televised documentaries on Saudi Arabia, Afghanistan, and Pakistan. Often they are occasions of public entertainment. Thousands of Muslims have been taped cheering as the punishments are meted out. To diminish sexual desires, some Muslims practice female genital mutilation, circumcision of the clitoris. This invasive procedure usually ceremoniously takes place just prior to puberty. – *In compassionate societies child labor laws have been in place for more than one hundred and fifty years. Slavery is an unacceptable and prosecutable offense in every Christianized nation. The ultimate goal of Western criminal codes is rehabilitation rather than mutilation. Anyone that intentionally performs a surgical procedure that diminishes the quality of life is liable for suit and prison internment.*

License to riot and loot

There is something virulent about the nature of Islam that incites its adherents to violence. This phenomenon is not restricted to Arab Muslims. If authority figures of Christian democracies utter even a hint of disrespect for Mohammed or the Quran, Mullahs start issuing death decrees. Violent riots ensue in every nation that has a significant Muslim population - Indonesia, Pakistan, India, Africa, and the Middle East alike. At the conclusion of the war for Iraq's freedom, thousands of its citizens began to loot and burn government facilities. Most would grant a temporary dispensation for this when the years of frustrating repression are taken into consideration. But, the looting included the shops of their hard-working fellows, libraries, and even medical equipment from the rooms of hospitalized patients. - *The citizens of free societies do not make a habit of demonstrating their displeasure over religious issues by rioting. Riots rarely occur, and when they do, they are commonly restricted to specific sections of cities rather than entire cities. Those rioting seldom loot the establishments of their fellows. It is unheard of for even the most calloused to loot medical devices from the rooms of patients that need them for survival.*

Geneva Convention defiance

Islam is unique in that it routinely encourages practices that would never be considered by spiritually sensitive people of other faiths. Women and children are used as human shields in battle. It is not unusual for boys as young as six years of age to be conscripted for wartime service. Adolescent boy and girls are celebrated for decisions to become homicide bombers. Muslims are known to utilize Red Crescent ambulances to transport troops and munitions. Hospitals are commonly used as command posts for combatants. Islamic regimes make a habit of killing the wounded of opposing forces and disposing of bodies without forwarding information about the fate of their victims. The various terrorist groups that operate in Israel often mutilate dead Israeli military personnel beyond recognition. - *The Geneva Convention was designed to protect non-combatants, the wounded, those surrendering, and prisoners of war. It specifies that no one under the age of fifteen can be conscripted for war. It prohibits the use of medical care facilities to camouflage aggression. In addition, each nation must follow procedures to identify the dead and wounded of opposing forces and to send information to their families. All peace-loving nations that value fairness and the dignity of the human race make every effort to comply with the spirit and intents of its regulations.*

Distain for other religions

It is a well-known fact that after the Israelis reclaimed Jerusalem in the Six-Day War, they were faced with an exhaustive clean-up project at the site of Herod's temple. For years the local Muslim Arabs had been using the base of the Wailing Wall as a public toilet. This defilement was nothing less than an intentional assault on the Jew's spiritual history. The Italian journalist, Oriana Fallaci, authored a book entitled *Rage and Pride*. In vivid, vernacular terms she described how offended she was about immigrant Somali Muslims defiling the grounds of a cathedral in Florence, Italy. They stained the marble edifice with their urine and filled the exterior entrance to the Bishop's Baptistery with their excrement. – *This type of behavior is simply beneath the sense of common decency that most religious people possess. Even in times of war, the soldiers of civilized countries refrain from dishonoring the belief systems of others. They take great pains to preserve their enemy's houses of worship.*

Muslim brotherhood myth

During the past thirty years, Muslims have purposely killed more Muslims than the combined number of deaths inflicted by their non-Muslim enemies. Anyone that has kept up with Middle East events understands that the concept of the brotherhood of Islam is a myth. It does not become a talking point unless one of their nations is facing non-Muslim foes.

If Israel or the coalition against international terrorism happens to accidentally harm civilians, the Muslim world riots in protest. There have been no international Muslim protests over the numerous incidences in which Muslim terrorists purposely maimed and killed citizens of free societies. Muslim communities around the globe take it in stride when factions within Islam commit genocide against one another in Jordan, Syria, Afghanistan, Egypt, Algeria, Tunisia, Iraq and Iran.

The war between Iran and Iraq took around a million Muslim lives. On various occasions, Saddam Hussein butchered tens of thousands of his own countrymen. In 1970, King Hussein of Jordan got wind that the Palestinians were going to attempt to take a portion of Jordan as their homeland. In a military campaign that is now called "*Black September*", he sent troops into the refugee camps of Southern Jordan and Lebanon. It is estimated that as many as four thousand Palestinians perished in the assaults. The global Muslim community did not riot in protest of this atrocity against their displaced brethren.

During the month of February of 1982, it became apparent that Islamic extremists headquartered in Hama, Syria were mounting an effort to make Syria an Islamic-governed state. President Hafez al-Assad took decisively brutal action. He bombarded the city with artillery and then had it bulldozed into the appearance of a giant parking lot. Amnesty International estimates that from ten thousand to twenty-five thousand civilians were slaughtered in the siege. There were no reports of the Muslims in other nations crying out that this was a grievous injustice against innocent civilians. – *After times of armed conflict nations that are built on Judeo-Christian ethics feed and clothe displaced persons. They rebuild the nations of their former enemies. It is interesting to note that when natural disasters strike Muslim countries, one rarely sees mercy missions initiated from fellow Muslim nations rushing to their aid. There are no occurrences of relief efforts coming from Islamic societies when disasters strike non-Muslim countries. Whenever and wherever disasters occur, the world can depend upon the financial resources and the relief efforts of nations that are built on Judeo-Christian values. Relief is dispersed to all, regardless of their nationality or religion. It is apparent that Islam is as inept at fostering merciful compassion as it is in creating fruitful economic conditions within the nations it controls.*

Predictable unpredictability

Throughout this chapter, it has been emphasized that Islamics routinely do things that mystify non-Muslims. Perhaps, one of the major enigmas that the world is learning to associate with Islam is its predictable unpredictability. In Iraq, the Coalition forces liberated the Shiite Muslims to celebrate a holiday that had been forbidden under Saddam Hussein's rule for thirty years. To the shock of all, the celebrations included anti-Coalition chants as well those attributing greatness to Allah. This is very different from the gratitude that was expressed by the Europeans when the Allied forces liberated them from Hitler's regime. Another example is the ludicrous lies that were told by Iraq's Minister of Information in 2003. He continually asserted that the Coalition forces were nowhere near Baghdad. In reality US soldiers were taking showers in Hussein's palace several blocks away from the site where he conducted his interviews. During the thirteen hundred years since Mohammed appeared on the scene, the world has drastically changed. Technology records and transmits the statements of statesmen and the actions of the masses around the globe instantaneously via the Internet and televised broadcasts. This being the case duplicitous spokesmen are quickly exposed. Religions that spawn human rights infractions and riotous violence soon accumulate reputations that reflect their true colors. For Islam this means that it can no longer hide behind its academic's claims that it is a progressive religion of peace and tolerance.

There are two ancient sayings that may help explain what causes many Muslims to react in unreasonable ways. The first is a prophetic utterance from the book of Genesis (Gen. 16:12). The Angel of the Lord told Hagar of her son, Ishmael (father of the Arabs), *"He will be a wild donkey of a man; his hand will be against everyone and everyone's hand against him, and he will live in hostility toward all his brothers".* This falls into line with the second, which is an Arabic proverb: *"I against my brothers; I and my brothers against my cousins; I and my cousins against the world".* It is my conviction that both are activated by the negative spiritual dynamics of Islam rather than a genetic curiosity resident in all Arabs. The Christian Arabs of America and the Middle East demonstrate no evidence of the prophecy's and the proverb's imprints on their lives. However, whenever Islam is embraced by any nationality, including Arabs, significant portions begin to demonstrate the bizarre behaviors indicative of the ancient sayings.

Fox News and some reports published in periodicals gave details about the psychological warfare that the Coalition forces used against the Iraqis. The Coalition understood that it was important to understand the psychology of Arabic speaking Muslims. The military's Psy-Ops units wisely discerned that they had sexual pride issues. Men that would commit suicide to attain a paradise with scores of virgins and increased sexual strength would likely host numerous other quirks.

Pride and sex

Here are two curiosities that were uncovered. Pride compels them to demonstrate fierceness in battle by brandishing weapons and making boastful threats prior to any actual conflict. Unlike the leaders of western nations, Islamic statesmen frequently brandish weapons and fire them in public. The masses respond with glee and fire their weapons, giving no thought to those in other vicinities that might be injured as the bullets fall from the sky. The Psy-Ops response to this quirk was ingenious. Leaflets were dropped that encouraged them with a way to save face and return home as war heroes. When the enemy comes make an initial charge and fire a few shots. Then lay down your weapons, discard your uniforms and go home. Another tactic was used for those that insisted on continuing the fight from hidden positions. Taped messages in Arabic would be broadcast from mobile units. These taunted the warriors with insinuations that there were rumors questioning the extent of their stamina in sexual exploits. Both worked. Thousands fired a few shots, laid down their arms, and returned to their homes. Thousands of others blindly charged into target areas to revenge the insults to their sexual pride.

Valley of decision

If you are a Muslim, I know that the contents of this chapter have been painful and perhaps infuriating. You know that the behaviors that have been cited are not rare occurrences. If you are residing in a Western democracy, you likely immigrated to escape the stifling influences endemic with Islamic regimes. I entreat you not to dismiss that which has been stated by rationalizing that every religion undergoes periods of unbecoming policies. Most religions have modified their former abusive excesses. This was done to keep pace with universally accepted standards that demand respect for every individual's right to freedom of choice. Any spiritual discipline that habitually insults basic human dignities is at risk of falling into disfavor and becoming obsolete. The seeds one sows tend to reap multiplied crops of that which was sown. If we have been intolerant of others, vast numbers will be harsher with us.

Islam's current reputation is deplorable to the global community. At this juncture, liberal France is concerned with the growth of Islamic fundamentalism. Its interior minister, Nicolas Sarkozy, is threatening to expel any foreign Muslim religious leader who disseminates extremist propaganda. Should this occur, it could eventually escalate to include every foreign Muslim. Historically, it has happened to other groups, and history does repeat itself. If France provides a precedent, other democracies could follow suit. Many want to be rid of elements that have proved to be subversive. Without question, the propensity of Islam to assert its will on non-Muslim populations is becoming increasingly disconcerting within numerous countries.

Muslim friend, this generation is confronting you with two choices. These could easily determine the destiny of your children. One is, unite with other concerned Muslims and demand that your clerics enact a reformation of Islam. This reformation must abolish every vestige of the abhorrent practices that are mentioned in this article. Only this can nullify that which the global community has learned to expect from Islam. The second choice is surely the wiser. You are likely Islamic by birth rather than choice. Liberate yourself and your descendants by finding a religion that bears evidence of the blessings of God. Christians are not perfect, and Christendom certainly has its problems. But, between Islam and Christianity, when it comes to objective evidence of God's affirmation, Islam is overwhelmingly outweighed.

Finally, as you ponder these matters, there are questions that you must resolve. What is it about Islam that causes its adherents to engage in, or to routinely acquiesce to, practices that other religions find objectionable? Does the content of the Quran have a greater tendency to enhance people's compassion for their fellow man or their inclination for barbarism? Is there any objective evidence that God endorses Islam more than any other religion? If you had not been born into a Muslim family, would the overall quality of life demonstrated by the world's Muslim populations attract you to Islam?

Hopefully, you are willing to engage in an experiment that has transformed the lives of thousands of Muslims. Ask God the Father to reveal Jesus to you through the power of the Holy Spirit. An Egyptian who was the Amir of the Islamic terrorist group *Gamma Islameyya* did so. You can read his testimony in Abdullah Al Araby's book, *"Snatched from the Lion's Jaws"*. Jesus walked into his room, enshrouded in a glorious light, and declared, *"I am He for whom you have been searching"*. The man's life was revolutionized. Yours can be too. It is something wonderful, why shouldn't you experience it?

Chapter 8:
Was 9/11 God's Judgment?

There are difficult things in this life that we may never understand. Due to this, there are times when we cannot help questioning God in how He can allow evil, heinous actions to happen such as the Islamic terrorists striking America on September 11, 2001. Some people have decided the reason is because our nation has not repented of its departure from our traditional Judeo-Christian values. This doctrinal bent is belied by an objective comparison of America with the Christian nation of Switzerland. Few nations can equal Switzerland's history as a birthplace for God-centered thought and Christian values. In the Sixteenth Century, it was a center for the Protestant Reformation. It was also the birthplace of Calvinism, which greatly influenced many American denominations. The flag that flies over the country features a white cross on a red background, symbolizing the cross and blood of Jesus. Keeping in mind that God is not a respecter of persons, it would seem that if America has come under judgment for abandoning its Christian values, then Switzerland should incur similar reprisals (Acts 10:34). However, the Swiss express little concern about issues such as abortion, drug abuse, and pornography. Extra-marital affairs and premarital sex are commonplace. Most Swiss Protestant churches have pastors who are elected by state-controlled elections. It is rare to encounter a state-elected clergyman who will testify to a born-again experience. Church attendance is an equal rarity—less than 20% of the population attends religious services.

If we take the following information into consideration, it would appear that either the concept that national troubles equal God's judgment is false or somehow Switzerland has unfairly received a favored nation status with the Lord. The Swiss have not had a famine since 1845, and with the exception of an occasional avalanche, natural disasters are rare. Every man under the age of fifty is a militiaman who must have a gun and ammo in his home at all times, yet there are very few homicides. Incidences of terrorism are uncommon. When it does occur, it is normally minor isolated instances of foreign nationals harassing other foreign nationals living in Switzerland, as opposed to foreign nationals attacking Swiss citizens. The Swiss have been spared from combat in any war over the past one hundred years. Their inflation rate is less than 1%, and their unemployment rate in 2000 was 1.7%. Looking at it from this viewpoint, Switzerland, indeed, does seem as though it has a favored nation status with God, in spite of its departure from traditional Christian values.

However, the concept that God subtly orchestrates evil on a nation because of the lack of traditional morals is grossly inconsistent with the New Testament (Jam. 1:13). This inconsistency is also clearly demonstrated by the fact that both Israel and America have been attacked in the midst of periods when they had heightened devotion to God. We can all take comfort from the words of the Lord to Jerusalem as recorded in Isaiah 54:15 in the New International Version, wherein God disclaims responsibility for the potential for attacks against them: *"If anyone does attack you, it will not be my doing; whoever attacks you will surrender to you."*

Ancient Israel

During the First Century A.D., the inhabitants of the city of Jerusalem exemplified a commitment to Judeo-Christian values eclipsing anything that America has ever known. The majority of Jews observed the Sabbath and participated in the annual observances of Passover, Pentecost, and Tabernacles. Children prayed in school and were instructed from the Scriptures. Jewish fathers taught their sons a trade and their wives were stay-at-home moms. Adultery, premarital sex, and homosexuality were strictly forbidden, and offenders could incur the death penalty. The early Church enjoyed a period of monumental evangelism, and the Messianic Christian community of converts from Judaism numbered in the tens of thousands (Acts 21:20). Many Christians attended public prayer sessions daily at the Temple of Herod. In the evenings, they gathered in homes for prayer, teaching, and fellowship (Acts 2:42-3:1). These believers generously shared their resources with those in need and were circumspect in caring for widows (Acts 6:1-4). No one could charge that Jewish and Christian children of the First Century were subjected to any of the societal woes that we conservative Christians commonly decry. School violence, drug traffic, MTV, and online porno sites were nonexistent. The environment of Jerusalem would qualify as godly when placed alongside the standard of that which most conservative Christians would describe as an ideal society. Nonetheless, the exemplary values of the city's inhabitants did not exempt it from experiencing a terrifying assault.

In 70AD, Titus, the son of the Roman Emperor Vespasian, led a barbarous campaign against Jerusalem during Passover and Easter time when thousands of Christians and Jews had gathered from the Mediterranean world to celebrate the occasion. The siege lasted one hundred and thirty-four days during which time the temple was destroyed, six hundred thousand were butchered, and one hundred and fifteen thousand were deported as slaves. The streets of the city were lined with those who had been crucified. The only Jewish Christians surviving the atrocities were those who fled as refugees to the city of Pella, which is located in present day Jordan.

America's revivals

Across the Atlantic, America's history is also punctuated with numerous instances where tragic events have followed close on the heels of periods of renewed spiritual fervency. For example, a revival called the Great Awakening occurred between 1730 and 1750. During those years churchgoers came to a place of repentance and there were thousands of new converts. At this time, 80% of the population began to attend church. Twenty-five years later, the nation was embroiled in the Revolutionary war.

In 1806, the Cane Ridge revival hit the mountain communities of Tennessee and Kentucky. Crowds of twenty-five thousand traveled by foot and wagon from the southern and mid-Atlantic-states to attend brush arbor camp meetings. These gatherings were noted for an awesome atmosphere filled with prayers of repentance. While heaven's dew still rested on the thousands that had been transformed during the revival, the English attacked America and the War of 1812 began. Washington D.C. was put to flames and was nearly completely destroyed. In September 1857, a businessman by the name of Jeremiah Lanphier was anointed with a burden to lead his contemporaries in regular times of prayer. He began a businessmen's prayer meeting in an upper room of the Dutch Reformed Church in Manhattan. At the first meeting, only six people out of a population of one million showed up. However, by March of 1858, every church and public hall in downtown New York was filled with people meeting for prayer. A reporter who worked for the famous editor Horace Greeley visited twelve meetings in one hour and counted six thousand one hundred men attending them. A landslide of prayer began, which overflowed to the churches in the evenings. People began to be converted—ten thousand per week in New York City alone. The movement spread throughout New England with the church bells bringing people to prayer at eight in the morning, noon, and six in the evening. The revival raced up the Hudson and down the Mohawk. The end result was that in 1860, out of the nation's thirty million people, more than one million were converted to Christ. In 1861, while millions of Americans basked in the joys of renewed faith, the Confederates bombarded Ft. Sumter and the War Between the States began. Scores of cities were burned and countless homes were pillaged. Union and Confederate concentration camps housed over four hundred thousand prisoners of war under the cruelest of conditions, and six hundred twenty thousand men lost their lives as Americans fought their fellow Americans. The abuses of brother on brother were so severe that war crime trials were held after the war.

The Holy Spirit's subtle work

Using these examples of Israel and America, it is apparent that when nations have revivals, it is more likely to be a preparation for national trials rather than a guarantee of protection from tumultuous times.

Was the terrorist attack on the Twin Towers of N.Y. and the Pentagon in Washington, D.C. evidence of God's displeasure and His absence from the hearts of Americans? Categorically not! Hundreds of supposedly calloused policemen and firemen demonstrated the Spirit of Christ as they paid the ultimate sacrifice to rescue strangers (Jn. 15:13; Rom. 5:7-8). Hundreds of others worked tirelessly in the recovery efforts. Scores of secular corporations and thousands of individuals have given benevolence totaling over a billion dollars to aid the hurting. The Christ-like manner in which so many Americans have responded to this crisis is reminiscent of the days of the prophet Elijah. He cried out to God that he was the only one left in all of Israel who had not worshipped Baal and that the rest of the population who had were seeking his life (1 Kings 19:18, Rom. 11:2-6). The Lord told Elijah about seven thousand people, that the prophet knew nothing about, who had a heart for God that equaled his. For years, Christian media personalities and conservative believers have been voicing similar complaints to God and to one another. Their murmurings implied that they stood alone as God's persecuted standards of righteousness in the midst of a nation that has bent its knee to the gods of materialism and secular humanism. Perhaps the Lord is revealing that He has hundreds of thousands times seven thousand Americans whose hearts are sensitive to the Holy Spirit. They may not be active in organized religions; nonetheless, they have a relationship with God. The Lord promised that He would pour out His Spirit on all flesh (Acts 2:17). The mercy that Americans have demonstrated could be the evidence that God has been covertly pouring out dosages of His Spirit on secular humanistic flesh that many never suspected would be candidates to receive it.

Terrorism, a sign of the times

In addition, during the two thousand years since the first advent of Christ, there has been no biblical or historical evidence that the righteousness of a nation guarantees a hedge of impenetrable protection against natural disasters, wars, and the exploits of wicked men who would cause the hearts of many to quake in fear. To the contrary, Jesus said that wars, natural disasters, and various forms of troublesome events would continue until His second advent (Luke 21:8-11, 26, Mk. 13:7-8). This is one of the reasons

His coming is called the blessed hope (Titus 2:13). Only His personal presence can end the adversities of this present age.

Could this tragedy have been avoided had more Christians been in a mode of repentance and prayer for America? Most likely not! In the quarter of a century prior to September 11, there were more Americans praying for the nation than at any other time in its history. A ministry called *Intercessors for America* was founded in 1974, and since then, hundreds of related prayer and repentance movements have been organized. People are praying in every level of national and state governments and among the country's general population. During the late 90s, the *Campus Crusades for Christ* founder, Dr. Bill Bright, led a prayer movement that emphasized the value of praying during forty-day fasts. It is estimated that one hundred thousand North American believers committed themselves to prayer and individual forty day fast. At this writing, more than a thousand churches nationwide join *Mahesh Chavda Ministries* of Charlotte, NC in weekly all-night prayer vigils. Many of the aforementioned organizations have routinely engaged in prayers of spiritual warfare in efforts to thwart the eventuality of attacks by Islamic terrorists.

America has never been God's holy nation

Both the Old and the New Testaments encourage believers to pray for their nations and their respective governments (Joel 2:12-32, 1 Tim 2:1-4). For example, God told Israel, through Solomon, that if they would humble themselves and pray, He would heal their land (2 Chron. 7:11-22). However, the United States cannot fully claim this promise that God gave to ancient Israel. It was given specifically to Jews who were under the Law of Moses and inhabitants Israel. Furthermore, there are no promises that dictate any nation will be exempt from the prophetic calamities that will occur on the planet as the end-time approaches.

It is less than prudent for clergymen and hyper-religious congregants to randomly apply Old Testament passages, relating to God's judgments and His promises of protection, to contemporary situations, that were specifically meant for ancient Israel. Although God has not changed in His character and loving care for mankind, His manner of dealing with us has (Mal. 3:6, Heb. 1:1-2). Many theologians agree that the Scriptures reveal at least two differing major periods of God's dealings with nations and men (Eph. 3:2; 1 Cor. 9:17 KJV): the Mosaic dispensation and the Christian dispensation. In each, respectively, there is the potential to experience both the goodness and severity of God (Rom. 11:22). Ancient Israel was a theocracy under the Mosaic dispensation in which the nation's government and religion were inseparable. The surrounding countries had similar theocratic governmental administrations that were under the influence of idolatrous religions. Israel was divinely commissioned to example the power and love of Jehovah to the surrounding societies. When it was singular in its devotion to the Lord, it prospered, and its prophets, like Jonah, were used to call other nations to repentance and to the worship of Jehovah (Jonah 3:4-10). When Israel embraced idolatry and national practices that were in direct conflict with God's laws, she reaped God's wrath.

The Church is His holy nation

The Christian dispensation, however, is far different. Since the resurrection of Christ, no earthly nation has ever served as God's singular representative to the earth in the same manner that Israel once did. The nations that are called Christian nations have various forms of democratic rule rather than theocratic rule. The

Church is now God's holy theocratic nation (1 Pet. 2:9). Its citizens are of every ethnicity and are scattered as ambassadors among the nations of the earth (2 Cor. 5:20). If the Church remains devoted to Jesus and represents His heart to the unconverted, it will be blessed (Prov. 14:34). If it embraces idolatry and accepts sinful practices as policy, it will be judged (1 Pet. 4:17, 1 Cor. 10:1-12). America, and other nations, will experience the calamities that are indicative of the end times. These calamities could be compared to the power of gravity that God set in motion at creation. If a person stumbles and breaks a limb, it does not indicate that God spontaneously played a part in their fall. The potential for natural and man-made disasters was set in motion in the earth due to the sin of Adam. When nations or individuals are traumatized by tragedies, it is not an inevitable signal that they have invoked the wrath of the Almighty. In most instances, these things occur simply because they have the potential to do so.

Regardless of what the hyper-religious discontents say about the state of the American Church, God is still using us. Our members provide the finances for evangelism and mercy missions throughout the earth. Our musicians still write the choruses of praise and worship that the whole world sings. Clergymen who hastily correlate disasters and the pain of others with God's judgment are doing a disservice to the cause of Christ. The Holy Spirit often heals and draws people to Jesus during periods when hearts have been sensitized through pain and misfortune. We will make His job far easier if we represent God as One who heals the broken-hearted rather than one that crushes bruised lives (Isa. 42:1-3; Luke 4:18).

The End

Other Books by Jim Croft

The Heritage Factor - Uncovers the life influencing powers in your spiritual and family heritage

Heaven on the Links - A devotional for golfers featuring tips, stories, and practical insights into how the game correlates with biblical concepts

Faith's Decision for the Abundant Life - Reveals how to lock into the flow of God's abundance

Charismatic Superstitions & Misconceptions - Unravels 75 confusing contemporary Christian doctrines

Dysfunctional Doctrines of the Hyper-Religious - Exposes where the Christian Conservative Right has gone astray

For more information on these books contact jcroft8942@adelphia.net or www.pccchurch.org/jc_ministries.htm

CPSIA information can be obtained at www.ICGtesting.com
Printed in the USA
BVOW07s1406201113

336834BV00002B/405/P